ORGANIZE YOUR HOME!

SIMPLE ROUTINES FOR MANAGING YOUR HOUSEHOLD

ORGANIZE YOUR HOME!

SIMPLE ROUTINES FOR MANAGING YOUR HOUSEHOLD

RONNI EISENBERG WITH KATE KELLY

NEW YORK

ISBN 0-7868-8382-0

Revised Edition
10 9 8 7

Design by Robert Bull Design

CONTENTS

This book is dedicated
to all of our wonderful readers and clients
who constantly inspire us to create
new and better ways to organize!

ORGANIZE YOUR HOME!

SIMPLE ROUTINES FOR MANAGING YOUR HOUSEHOLD

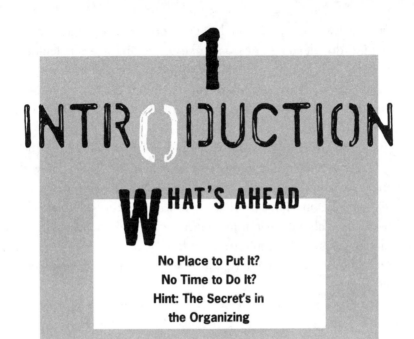

1
INTRODUCTION

WHAT'S AHEAD

No Place to Put It?
No Time to Do It?
Hint: The Secret's in
the Organizing

"How do you do it?" is a question I'm frequently asked when friends and acquaintances visit my home. Because I have a husband, three young children (two of them twins), two dogs, and my own business, they often add: "You're so calm, and your home is so organized. What's your secret?"

I've written *Organize Your Home!* to share my secrets with you, because I know from experience that the busier your life becomes—and the more responsibilities you have—the more important it is to be organized. If I weren't, how would I get through my days without leaving behind dry cleaning, misplacing keys, arriving late for dental appointments, and generally coping with the chaos that can arise in a busy household. Because I am organized, I can get to appointments on time and find what I'm looking for. In addition, everything I need to take care of gets done.

Being organized is something I count on: I expect to find the library books so I don't have to waste time looking for them; I know that I won't have to run out to the grocery store daily because my kitchen is well stocked; and I'm sure that if the weather turns suddenly cold (or hot) I'll be able to switch my outfit for the day in an instant. If I didn't have this well-organized home base from which to operate, I would feel overwhelmed, guilty, and forever apologetic for not getting things done.

Organize Your Home! is going to help you organize **your** home—and even stay calm through the process. Within the book you'll find hundreds of simple, do-it-yourself suggestions for attics and garages and closets and kitchens. There's also information on how to sort through your mail, organize a dinner party, set up a home computer, and more. In addition, I have two organizing principles that will help you get started.

ORGANIZING PRINCIPLE NO. 1

Everything must have a place. Sounds simple, doesn't it? But look around you. The reason you feel disorganized is because many things don't have specific places where they belong.

As a professional organizer, I visit many homes. When I meet with a client for the first time, I'll typically find these sorts of things with "no home":

—Mom's birthday present, which needs to be wrapped but won't be taken to her for a week

—A broken watch that has to be repaired

—A desk covered with unopened mail

—Papers related to work or a special project strewn or stacked on a table

—Unread magazines

—Items that need to be either mended or cleaned

—New clothes, with tags still attached, tossed over a chair, waiting to be put away

—Old clothes to be donated

—Lots and lots of photographs—anywhere and everywhere, but usually not in frames or albums

—And shopping bags, shopping bags, and more shopping bags—

filled with paraphernalia that needs to be taken care of someday once the client figures out what to do with it all

Stroll through your own home. Areas near the main door are generally very cluttered, and there is usually one room, sometimes the bedroom, sometimes a dumping room, where things just get stashed "until I have time . . ."

As you go through this book chapter by chapter, I'll tell you how to find places for all the clutter that has collected—unfiled papers, too many cookbooks, unsorted photos, gifts you don't want. You'll learn to weed out regularly instead of doing it once every few years. As you work, just keep in mind: you must find a place for **everything**, and then develop the habit of **putting away**.

ORGANIZING PRINCIPLE NO. 2

You must have a system for all household responsibilities. When I consult with people about the problems they are having, I find that there are five common mistakes people make when managing things around the house:

1. They don't write things down. (If you expect to **remember** all your appointments, you are going to slip up at some point; if you don't write down your questions to ask the doctor, you may forget.)

2. They let things pile up (laundry, unopened mail, unread magazines, home projects . . . the list goes on).

3. They let things run out (gift-wrapping supplies, grocery items, toothpaste, medicine . . .).

4. They don't finish what they start. (They start reorganizing the kitchen; or begin to put their photos in albums; or they begin to set aside things for a white-elephant sale . . . but something else comes up. If they do return to the project, it's like starting all over again, because they forget where they left off.)

5. They don't keep it up. It takes commitment and persistence to reach a goal. If you don't keep it up week to week, the clutter starts to creep back.

To start developing systems, think **routine**. People who exercise regularly generally have a specific time of day they do it, and many even exercise seven days a week, because they don't like to break the routine—it's easier to do it than to **think** about whether to do it.

The same is true for household systems. If it becomes habit, you'll find these tasks become a way of life: Wednesday is invariably grocery-shopping day, Thursday you change the beds, Friday is one of two laundry days, and you're so accustomed to handling your mail daily that it rarely piles up. You'll actually save time because you won't be indecisive anymore: "Should I really go out to the grocery in the rain, or should I wait until tomorrow?" You'll do the tasks without thinking about it, leaving your mind free to plan other things.

Having a system for all of your day-to-day responsibilities will free you to do special things like spending good time with your family instead of worrying about all the things you should have gotten done.

Getting organized is a constant process, not a onetime goal. It takes daily effort to get your chores accomplished and be ready for the tasks that need to be done tomorrow. Family illness or difficulties, last-minute projects at work, or even a vacation can throw off your routine. Don't get discouraged. Refer to *Organize Your Home!* again if you need to, and otherwise just keep on course. If you have the will to get organized, then you'll learn how to stay that way, too.

2

THE ATTIC, BASEMENT, AND GARAGE

WHAT'S AHEAD

Sorting and Categorizing
Storage Ideas
Typical Storage Collections
Storage Items: Basement and
Garage
Garage Items Only

If your attic and basement are like most, they're jumbles of "stuff." The kids' sleeping bags have been tossed onto your suitcases, which sit beside the picnic basket you've never used, which resides beside the plastic cutlery you do use—once or twice a year. The garage is likely a dusty collection of bikes, yard equipment, old furniture, and miscellaneous household items.

Attics, basements, garages, and, for apartment dwellers, storage bins are repositories for items that fall into the category of "Well, someday I might need it." To organize these spaces, three steps are necessary:

1. Resolve to toss out the things you really haven't looked at for years.
2. Sort and categorize the remainder.
3. Organize and label what you're keeping.

Sorting and Categorizing

- Start when you have several hours to devote to getting the project under way. If you haven't finished after the first session, the remainder of the work can be done in smaller blocks of time.

SMART TIP

- Asking for help from other family members is tempting, but think carefully before you include them. Is your spouse a pack rat? If so, you don't need help!

- In fairness to the family, announce that you are undertaking this project. Your son who has just taken his own apartment may want to come and retrieve all of his college texts before they are given away. (If he chooses to store them at his place, that's fine. It's **your** basement, attic, or garage you're trying to clean.)

- Gather several large trash bags and some boxes. The bags are for items you're throwing out. Box No. 1 should be for items you want to donate or sell at a tag sale. (If you plan to do both, set aside two boxes.) Additional boxes will be necessary for sorting items by category. (Create the categories and label as you go along.)

- Also get out:
  —Stepladder
  —Vacuum
  —Cleaning rags
  —Spray cleaner
  —Leaf blower (for garage clean-out), if you have one

- If the area is very dusty, work in rubber or cotton gloves to protect your hands.

- Choose a starting spot along a wall, and work systematically. You're going to have to evaluate everything that is stacked, stuffed, or lounging against the wall. This won't be too difficult with most items, but some, such as a box of family letters, might be better off saved for a more careful sorting. (When you do go through them, you should still toss what now seems unnecessary and categorize and neatly store what you save.)

- Be hardhearted about tossing. The beaters for a mixer you no longer own? Toss them. The toddler wading pool last used the summer of '88? Give it away. And the broken wooden ornament that you haven't fixed for three Christmases will probably never be glued. Toss it.

Important!

- Set up categories as you go. Jigsaw puzzles that someone will work again deserve special storage. Put the puzzle boxes in a larger box and label it "puzzles."

- Keep working until all your belongings have been dusted off, sorted, and categorized.

STORAGE IDEAS

Once you've sorted your belongings, you may find some of these storage units will work for you:

Old kitchen cabinets: People who have had a kitchen redone often ask the workers to install the old cabinets in the basement or garage. This creates terrific storage for all types of things: the oversized serving dishes (and twenty-five-cup coffee maker) you use when company comes; extra glassware; large pitchers; seasonally used cookie tins and cake covers; as well as miscellaneous items such as holiday decorations. The drawers come in handy for extra batteries, light bulbs, shoe polish, tools, etc.

Wardrobe units: For holding out-of-season clothing.

Metal cabinets: Office-supply stores sell five- and six-foot-tall metal cabinets that offer a wealth of storage in a dust-free space. Measure ceiling height before ordering.

File cabinets: These are perfect for old financial records, tax records, and dead storage. (Current files belong in a more accessible part of the house. See Chapter 6, Household Files.) Because this information will be referred to infrequently, you don't need state-of-the-art cabinets. Buy secondhand, or price-shop for the most economical ones you can find.

Special carpentry: Hire a carpenter to build some rough shelving for you, or put up sheetrock to create a separate storage room.

- Many of the items that are housed in attics, basements, and garages are large and awkward. But even these hard-to-store pieces (skis, for example) should look as if they are put away. Add a rack on one wall for skis. Balls, bats, and other sports paraphernalia can be contained in a large bin. Assess what will work best for what you have.

- As you select and arrange the storage units that seem best, keep in mind how the space will be used. In a basement, there might be one area with exercise equipment; a carpentry and painting work space on the far wall; and a pool table in the middle of the room. One family has a walk-in attic, where their children's dress-ups are stored. Though most of the attic is storage, the family put down a rug in front of the dress-up trunk and set out a couple of chairs. The effect is a little "parlor" for play.

TYPICAL STORAGE COLLECTIONS

Here are some of the collections I generally find in the nether reaches of a home and what I suggest about each.

Hand-me-downs: While saving boots, winter coats, jeans, and any clothing in good condition for siblings makes perfect sense, be selective. Stained clothing looks terrible when you pull it out in a few years, and if too many years pass between wearers, items like tights and socks lose their elasticity. Box and label—"Mary, age 5, summer clothes"—what you save.

Out-of-season clothing: To simplify switching seasonal clothing, out-of-season clothes should best be stored in a convenient extra closet in the main part of your house or apartment. However, if you must use the attic or basement, invest in a wardrobe or have a carpenter build a closet there for you. The clothing should be hung neatly in a dust-free environment so that you needn't clean or wash everything again when you get it out.

Luggage: The attic, basement, or separate storage area in the garage is the perfect place for luggage. Keep only the bags you really use, and consider whether they can be stored within one another. (Your carry-on tote should fit conveniently within your regular-sized suitcase.) Within your suitcase, keep the tissue paper, plastic garment bags, shoe bags, and any extra toiletry bags.

Have two deep shelves built, custom-measured for your family's luggage. Cover the bags with an old sheet to keep dust-free.

Mementoes: Even boxes of mementoes need to be evaluated now and then. Most people save too much. A senior prom can be documented by a few photographs; don't save the pressed flowers from the corsage (that you don't know what to do with anyway). And the ticket stubs from the Tower of London? Unless they are cleverly added to a travel journal or photo album, they really aren't worth keeping. And what about the four copies of the newspaper in which your daughter's picture appeared? Newsprint deteriorates quickly, so have the picture copied onto acid-free paper, label it, put it in a scrapbook, and toss out all the newspapers. Nursery-school artwork? Keep a few representative pictures, and add notes about why you kept it: "Scott's first attempt to print his name." Once you've decided what's worth keeping, move it out of the basement, attic, or garage. The dampness of basements, the heat variations of attics, and the inevitable dirt that comes into garages all can contribute to deterioration. Make room for keepsakes in the climate-controlled part of the house, perhaps on an upper shelf of a closet.

Old furniture: It should be saved when it's in usable condition and meets some of the following criteria:

—You can use it for storage in the attic or basement. (Old dressers or bookshelves can be very handy.)

—You are planning to create a basement recreation room.

—Your child will need to furnish a college room or his or her own apartment within the next year or two.

—It's a family heirloom or a very lovely piece of furniture—you just don't have space for it right now.

Otherwise, pass it on. Donate it to a white-elephant sale; give it to a neighbor; sell it at a yard sale.

Old books and magazines: Do you really think you'll ever look at your college psychology text again? And of what value is that high school geography book when the world has changed so much in recent years? Novels and nonfiction you've enjoyed should be saved selectively. Classics or books you loved and might read again should be shelved, preferably in the main part of the house. Other books should be shared. Pass them on to a friend or donate them for the library's book sale. (Call the library to see if there are restrictions on what they'll accept.) As for all the *National Geographics* . . . if you have the makings of a real collection, get them into a climate-controlled part of the house where people can see and enjoy them. Otherwise, give them away. If your daughter has to do a report on the femur's native habitat, you can get a copy of the article at the library.

Pictures and paintings: Will you (or any family member) ever want to hang them again? If so, choose a spot where you can store the paintings upright. Use sheets or old blankets to cover and separate each painting.

STORAGE ITEMS: BASEMENT AND GARAGE

Houses that lack attics and basements generally use the garage for general household storage. Here are items you might find in either the basement or garage:

Aquariums, bird cages, etc.: If the first time you set up an aquarium all the fish died, is this really the hobby for you? As for getting another bird . . . If you really aren't the type to make the bird cage into a folk-art addition to your home, then pass it on.

Baby equipment: Parents expecting to add to the family should cover and store these items neatly, and grandparents who have frequent young visitors will want to as well. As for keeping your child's crib or high chair to pass on to his or her family later on, forget about it, unless it's a family heirloom. Give it to another family now.

Bags, boxes, tins: Just because you might need a shopping bag, a mailing box, or a cookie tin one day doesn't mean you need to save fifty of them. Save a few in good condition, and keep the collection pared down. Hardware stores and organizing shops sell special wire holders for bags. You can also use one large bag to store the others, folded. Recycle those you don't need.

Paint: Paint left over from a recent house repainting should be labeled (as to room and whether it was wall color or trim) and preserved. (Colors from paint-jobs-past should be disposed of as specified by your community.) Closed storage is ideal. If not, store paint cans on shelves.

Sports paraphernalia: You used to ski and you are saving your skis for your daughter. Don't bother. Equipment such as this has improved through the years, and you'll be doing your child a favor by letting her learn on up-to-date equipment. What about the old tennis racquet? It will probably need to be restrung. Drop by a tennis shop and ask whether the racquet is worth the added expense. Otherwise, sports equipment should be stored together, as neatly as possible.

Tools: If you just keep a few tools around for emergencies, a simple toolbox will be perfect for your needs. A good hardware store can sell you the box along with the bare necessities for emergency home repairs. A family member who is handy will likely want a real workbench. Some benches have ready-made slots to hold tools, or you may want to add a peg board behind the workbench to hang tools. Using a black magic marker, outline each tool in the place you want it hung.

That way, family members can tell at a glance where everything belongs.

If you have a collection to clean out, start by sorting and categorizing. Gather and put away in a workbench or tool kit the hammers, screwdrivers, and hand drills you own. If you have large power tools, store them in a closed cupboard or in a separate box. Now sort the miscellany. Coffee cans, properly labeled, are good for storing nails, screws, nuts and bolts. Or invest in a special organizer at the hardware store.

Miscellany: Awkward items such as picnic baskets, sleeping bags, and the aquarium you finally decided to keep should be placed neatly on shelves. Items such as picnic cutlery should be stored in labeled boxes, bags, or storage-unit drawers. Papers for dead storage or financial records belong in a file cabinet. Just keep working through the miscellany. Each item should be evaluated. Ask:

    1. Should I keep it?

    2. What's the best way to bag or box it?

Then label it and put it away.

GARAGE ITEMS ONLY

Bicycles: If you have a spacious garage, create a bike "parking lot." Bike helmets should be hung on the handlebars, or stored on a shelf nearby. If bikes are not used regularly—or if space is at a premium—

hang the bikes on the wall. Special hooks for this purpose are available from hardware stores and bicycle shops.

Gardening hand tools: Hand tools and gardening gloves should be kept in a plastic caddy like the ones sold in hardware stores. This keeps everything handy so that if you have just a few minutes to work in the garden you have all your tools together to do so. Within the garage, it is nice to have a closed cupboard where you can store the caddy and related items such as flower pots and fertilizer and other seasonal items.

Hoses: Hose caddies that store the hose rolled up are invaluable for keeping the lawn tidy during the summer; in winter, bring the entire caddy into the garage for storage.

Lawn-care products: Buy or save a large trash can (with cover) for storing bags of lawn fertilizer or other products such as wood chips.

Long-handled yard equipment: rakes, brooms, snow shovels, etc. These should be hung. Mount a board on which special holders can be installed for these items.

Recycling holders: Each community's separation requirements are different, but select storage units that can hold what you save. If you take recyclables to the dump, be certain that the containers you choose fit in the car.

3

CALENDARS AND ELECTRONIC ORGANIZERS

WHAT'S AHEAD

Selecting the Calendar That's Right for You
Using Your Calendar Effectively
The Family Wall Calendar
Electronic Organizers and Personal Digital Assistants

A calendar is the key to an organized life, and while I meet few people who don't have calendars, I meet many who fail to use them properly. Clients' complaints are **always** along these lines: "Well, I always play tennis on Fridays at 6 P.M. Why would I need to write that down?"

By failing to note all her appointments on her daily calendar, this particular client is making three mistakes:

1. She thinks she'll **never** forget about that Friday-at-6 P.M. game, but one day she will. We've all booked dental and medical appointments for times when, if we'd given it any thought, we couldn't possibly get there.

2. She can't assess her schedule. Only by "painting a picture" of your complete week can you accurately assess your time. If you're combing through your calendar looking for a day when you could make a short out-of-town trip, you're less likely to choose Friday if you've got that 6 P.M. appointment noted down.

3. She's overburdening herself. The point of a calendar is to get everything written down so you needn't remember it. If you develop the habit of **always** noting your commitments, you'll never again be plagued with that uncomfortable feeling of, "Did I remember to write that down?" In the future, you'll know that you did.

So whether you ultimately have a paper calendar or an electronic organizer, make certain that you enter **every**thing **every** day.

SELECTING THE CALENDAR THAT'S RIGHT FOR YOU

- Choose one daily calendar that works for you. Some people keep one calendar at the office and another at home, but invariably they slip up—they get harried and forget to transfer something from one calendar to the other, and the result is missing an important appointment. By selecting a good calendar that is easy to carry with you, you'll never have to worry about what you might have forgotten to enter.

- Whether your calendar is a page-a-day or a week-at-a-glance, a good calendar should be:

  — Small enough to carry with you at all times.

  — Large enough to provide space to record appointments and activities, to make notes (such as questions to ask at your next appointment), and to keep a list of errands and projects to accomplish that day.

USING YOUR CALENDAR EFFECTIVELY

- **Write down everything.** Don't clutter your mind with having to remember that you're meeting your parents for dinner on Sunday

---

and that your Saturday afternoon squash game has been moved up an hour.

- When recording an appointment, write down the address, telephone number, and directions in the space next to the appointment. When it's time to go to the appointment you have all the information you need at your fingertips.

- Every few days, review with your spouse any new items on each of your calendars. You can coordinate on the times when you'll be together and plan accordingly for times when you're each going your separate ways.

THE FAMILY WALL CALENDAR

A family wall calendar is the only exception to the one-calendar rule, and the reason for this exception is easy: Family organization is much smoother if there is one central location where all family members can record their own dates and check the whereabouts of other family members. A quick glance at the family wall calendar should show that not only do you have to get Billy to the orthodontist at 4 P.M., but you also have to be sure you're back in time to get Sarah to her piano lesson at 4:45 P.M.

- Purchase a good-sized (I like 17 x 22-inch) calendar to hang in a central location near a telephone. In most homes this is the kitchen.

- Each family member should be assigned a personal color. Select another color for recording family activities. That way it's easy to spot who is doing what on any given day.

- When a child becomes old enough to start taking responsibility for his or her own plans, it's time for him to write it down on his own.

- Write down your own plans when they affect the family: "Mom working late" on Tuesday will let everyone know your where-abouts; "visit Grandma" in Sunday's box will remind family members not to make any conflicting plans for that day.

- Be sure to write down all regular commitments such as dance class or music lessons.

- Check the wall calendar daily to see if there is information there you need to add to your personal calendar. You don't want to schedule a meeting at the time you promised to pick up your son and his friends at the mall.

ELECTRONIC ORGANIZERS AND PERSONAL DIGITAL ASSISTANTS

More and more people are asking, "Should I get an electronic organizer?"

While an increasing number of people are falling in love with these digital assistants, I continue to recommend that you use what works best for you. The electronic organizers have many capabilities that can't be duplicated with a paper-based system: In addition to serving as calendar and telephone directory, they can act as an alarm clock, pager, calculator, note pad, expense log, game board, e-mail retrieval system, and Web browser. Nonetheless, many people still prefer the dependability of being able to put their hands on a paper calendar that is still perfectly capable of doing its job—keeping track of the who, what, when, and where of our daily lives.

Formerly considered an executive toy, these electronic organizers vary widely. One style, the **personal information manager**, is a hand-held electronic device designed to keep phone lists, addresses, and appointments, but these systems generally are more limited in capacity because they do not interface with a computer. A more advanced style is actually considered to be a **palmtop computer** (also known as a "personal digital assistant"), and this type is much more sophisticated. It operates much like a personal computer, and it can be connected to a fax machine or an online service or linked to your computer for information exchange. Palmtop computers function like organizers, keeping phone numbers and appointments, but they often include word processing and spread sheet capabilities and sometimes wireless faxing and data reception. Keep in mind that the more bells and whistles the unit has, the more likely it is to be somewhat ungainly to carry around with you.

If you're in the market for some type of electronic organizer, here are some points to consider:

- Evaluate for weight and convenience.

- Ask how the information is entered. Most have a keyboard; some of the newer ones are designed to read your handwriting when written with a special pen on the screen.

- Many keyboards are quite small so evaluate them for ease of use "Hunt and peck" typists seem to mind the shrunken keyboards the least.

- Compare screens. Make sure the one you select is easy to read. Those that feature backlighting tend to be more versatile.

- Ask what software interfaces with the unit you're considering.

One primary advantage of the palmtop computers over the smaller organizers is the back-up capacity. Because the palmtop can interface with your desktop computer, you can print out information from it and run a full back-up of the data as well. If the thought of losing your calendar/organizer makes your blood run cold, then restrict your search to the more advanced palmtop computers.

While many are perfectly happy with their paper-based calendars, there is no doubt that these little hand-held gadgets have a lot to offer. If you think you'll use several of its features then you really ought to give it a try.

4

CLOSETS
AND DRAWERS

WHAT'S AHEAD

Five Steps to Reorganizing Your Closets
Bedroom Closets
Out-of-Season Storage
Drawers
Accessories: How to Store
Jewelry
Linen Closets
Hall Closets

When it comes to closets, my profession is not for the weak of heart. From the depths of clothes closets, I've pulled out unworn designer clothes (in multiples, with tags still attached!) and tripped over skis. I've had many clients who pulled out one slipper, only to explain that the other one is "in there, somewhere."

One friend has a walk-in hall closet where she stores everything. It's primarily a coat closet, but she also uses it for art supplies, puzzles, skates, and games, and there's generally a basketball rolling around on the floor when you open the door. The other day I returned some baby clothing to her. (Her youngest is now five.) I couldn't help but laugh when she took the bag of clothing I'd borrowed, marched directly to this "all-purpose" closet, and put it in—one more hurdle to overcome when she's running the "Let's get our coats" obstacle race.

Like my friend, most people have a love/hate relationship with their closets. They love to stuff in everything they ever owned, bought, or borrowed, but hate it when they can't find what they're looking for.

It's time to bring everything out from behind closed doors when:

—Stored items are stuffed in too tightly. (Imagine squeezing a size-14 body into a size-8 dress!)

—Clutter covers the floor.

—The shelves are about to collapse.

—You can't see it and you can't find it!

TO HAVE A PERFECT CLOSET, ITEMS MUST BE:

- visible
- accessible
- pared down

Now it's time to get started!

FIVE STEPS TO REORGANIZING YOUR CLOSETS

STEP ONE: Weed Out

- Whether you're cleaning out a linen closet, coat closet, or the closet where you keep your clothes, the process is the same. Go through item by item, and decide what to keep and what to give away.

Coats, clothes, hats, and accessories: If you haven't used or worn it in over a year, if it's frayed or worn-looking, if it brings back bad memories, or if you never liked it to begin with, give it away. As for those items you've kept "in case they come back in style . . ." If there's not a chance in a million they will (and if they did, would they still fit?), then pass those clothes on today.

Store only the current season's clothing in your primary clothes closet. Some oversized closets can accommodate extra clothes storage, but as a general rule, you're better off setting aside all out-of-season items to store elsewhere. We'll discuss how and where later in the chapter.

Linens: Pull out frayed or worn-looking sheets, towels, and extra blankets. If you have a child going to camp or college, set aside the least worn of these and store them (labeled) in the basement or attic, or on an upper shelf of the child's room until the date they are needed. Old sheets can also be used to cover out-of-season clothing or, in the attic or basement, to cover paintings or other large items that should be kept dust-free. Old blankets can be set aside for picnics, and old towels make great rags. Cut them up and save them.

Other belongings: As you go through other items, ranging from sports equipment and jigsaw puzzles to holiday ornaments and extra light bulbs, ask these questions:

1. Do I still use it?
2. Is there a better way to box and label it before putting it away?
3. Is this closet the best place to store it?

STEP TWO: Evaluate Exactly What You Need to Store in Each Closet

- Now that you've sorted through the contents, you need to decide exactly what each closet must accommodate:

  —In a clothes closet: How many separates? How many suits? How many dress-length items? Just a few shoes? Do you need to keep sweaters in the closet, or do you have a bureau in the room? What about accessories?

—In other closets: Are you storing sports equipment? Board games? Out-of-season coats? If so, how much space is needed? In the linen closet are you putting away three sets of towels or six?

—Make notes about what you are storing in each closet. Be sure it makes sense. For example, storing guest linens in the upstairs linen closet when the guest bedroom is downstairs is inconvenient. Is there an upper shelf in the guest-bedroom closet where the linens could be placed so they'll be nearer where they are used?

STEP THREE: Evaluate Your Closet Space

- How large is it? (Note measurements.) What shape?

- Are the shelves accessible? Could shelves be added? Sometimes hanging poles can be lowered 6 to 8 inches, giving you space for an additional shelf at a more convenient height.

- What about the hanging space? Is it deep, meaning that hanging one pole behind another makes sense? Or is it particularly high, so that out-of-season clothing might be stored on a pole above the regular one?

- Are the doors usable for storage? (Swinging doors are; sliding doors aren't.)

- Can you see the contents? Will lighting help?

STEP FOUR: Look for Organizing Solutions

- Are built-ins the answer? If you expect to stay in your home over the next few years, hire a closet company to come in and design the space so it meets your needs. They can add shelves, extra rods, and various apparatus that can help make any closet a dream.

- Visit a closet shop or the closet department in a major department store. There are a number of modular drawer, shelf, and basket storage systems that adapt well to existing spaces. Some home centers even have do-it-yourself closet kits. One of these systems may be just right for you.

- Or choose from storage aids, such as stackable bins, hatboxes, pull-out shelves, ready-made drawer units, and spinning caddies, which can be used to make your closet space more functional. (Read on to learn ways to use the various organizing units.)

STEP FIVE: Basic Reorganizing

- Set aside several hours to work. Have on hand rags, spray cleaner, and the vacuum.

- Clear the space and remove any shelving or poles that are wrong for you. Give the closet a thorough cleaning.

- Now is the time to paint or wallpaper, or carpet the floor, if you want to improve the look of the entire closet.

- Paint shelves with a high-gloss paint or polyurethane to make them easy to wipe clean. (Some polyurethane finishes need only a few hours to dry, so if you paint in the late afternoon, you could put things away the next day.)

- Install new shelving and poles (if necessary), put in hooks, and put into place any organizers.

- Purchase shelf dividers that clamp onto the shelf to create barriers between items. Handbags will stand erect and stacks of sweaters won't tumble over if they have dividers to lean against.

- A light in a closet is a must; one that turns on when the door is opened is a wonderful luxury.

- Invest in sturdy, well-designed hangers made of wood or plastic or covered in fabric. They'll help your clothes retain their shape longer and make it easier to keep the closet organized.

AS YOU ORGANIZE, ASK YOURSELF THESE QUESTIONS:

1. Are the most frequently used items at eye level?

2. Can I see everything easily? (Don't stash items behind other items.)

3. Can I reach what I need quickly and with a minimum of effort?

See below for specific suggestions for various types of closets.

BEDROOM CLOSETS

- If a closet must be shared by two people, each should have his or her own hanging and shelf space.

- If you have many separates, create space where you can double hang. Hire a carpenter (or a closet company) to divide your hanging space in half so that one part is preserved for longer clothing, and the other side can have an upper pole and a lower pole for separates.

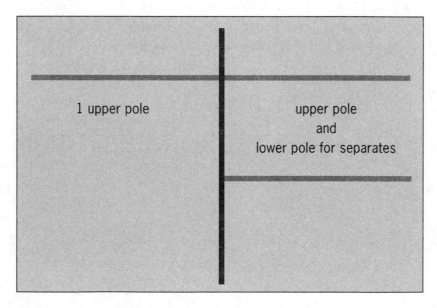

1 upper pole

upper pole
and
lower pole for separates

(Before final installation, be certain that the lower pole is high enough so that your clothes don't drag.) Then set it up with shirts and jackets on bottom (bulky items below) and shorts and pants or skirts above.

- Categorize clothing by both type and color. All shirts, slacks, vests, jackets, dresses, and skirts should be put in their own category, though matching sets should be hung together. Colors should run from dark to light. Once the clothing is categorized, you may realize that you really do have five pairs of black slacks. Next shopping trip, you can invest in another color.

- Frequently worn clothing should be hung so that it is accessible. Less frequently used items such as tuxedos, formal gowns, and cocktail dresses should be stored out of the way at the back or far side of the closet.

- Hooks are invaluable. Use them to hold bathrobes, nightgowns, and pajamas. Put up an extra hook to provide a temporary holding spot for the fresh-from-the-dry cleaner clothes you are putting away.

- On one side of the closet door, hang a full-length mirror so that you can check your appearance after dressing.

- Save space for a stepstool so that you have an easy way to reach upper shelves.

- If items will be stored in boxes or containers within the closet, be sure that everything is clearly labeled.

- For the oversized walk-in closet, consider:

    —Counter space to lay out jewelry and accessories as you're dressing

    —A bench that offers convenient seating when you're putting on shoes and socks

    —A dry-cleaner rotation-style clothing machine that provides a motorized system for bringing your wardrobe into view. These are available for the home but require a closet that is at least six by six.

    —A three-way mirror

HANGING TIPS

- Clothes need breathing space. Don't overcrowd; it causes wrinkles.

- Use sturdy hangers of good quality.

- After hanging, run your hand down the garment to make certain the article hangs properly (no twisted lapels or bunched sleeves).

- When hanging a suit or jacket, always empty all pockets.

- Hang delicate skirts (and suedes) inside out for extra protection. (Dresses and jackets should not be reversed because then the fabric would rub directly on the hanger.)

- Dresses hang best on a proper-size padded hanger.

- When hanging blouses or dresses, fasten, button, or zip to the neckline so they hang properly.

- Hang pants from the bottom, using a pants hanger, or fold the slacks over a hanger with a rounded bottom to lessen the crease that will settle in.

- Even if you've installed a light in your closet, it can be difficult to tell black from navy. Identify the color in good light and tie a colored (yellow?) ribbon around the neck of the hanger of everything navy. Then you'll know at a glance what color it is.

SMART TIP

H ANGING GONE WRONG

- Never store clothing in plastic. It keeps the clothes from "breathing" and can cause discoloration. Instead, use dark colored cloth garment bags.

- Don't hang sweaters; they sag. Instead, fold and store on a shelf.

- Avoid hangers designed to hold multiples (slacks, skirts, etc.). The clothes get bunched up and they wrinkle.

- Don't put away dirty clothing.

- Double-check hems and look for stains, missing buttons, and creases that need to be ironed out before the next wearing.

- And no matter what your friends say, your exerbike or stair climber is **not** the right place to hang clothing. Hang up outfits after you've worn them, and they'll last longer.

OUT-OF-SEASON STORAGE

To maintain a tidy clothes closet, you must switch clothing at the end of each of the major seasons.

- The ideal spot for storing out-of-season clothing is a well-ventilated closet in the regular part of the house, not in the attic or basement. Attic heat can cause hidden stains to become apparent. Basement dampness causes mildew.

- Clean everything before putting it away. (Moths look for food-saturated areas first.)

- For folded items such as sweaters and knits, use cedar chests or dust-free boxes. Add mothballs (look for pleasant-scented ones at specialty shops and in catalogs), but don't let mothballs touch clothing.

- Save shoe boxes to store out-of-season shoes. Label them or use transparent boxes so that shoes are easily identified.

- Keep cruise or ski wear together as an ensemble, complete with the appropriate handbags and shoes. When it's time to pack for your winter trip, everything will be organized and accessible.

WORTH THE TIME

- No place to store extra clothing at home? Look for a dry-cleaning establishment that offers boxed storage. The cleaner provides the box, and after you fill it up, the clothes are cleaned and stored until you're ready for them in four or five months.

- Furs should go to a furrier for storage in a controlled environment.

DRAWERS

Drawer contents tend to jumble easily because of the frequent shaking involved in opening and closing drawers. Because of this, they need to be particularly well organized:

- Going from top to bottom, organize drawers in the order you get dressed: i.e., underwear, undershirts, and socks would be in upper drawers, shirts and sweaters lower down.
- Buy a large supply of dividers, and customize your drawers.
- Keep like items together, and group by color.
- Store more frequently used items near the front of the drawers.
- Do not overstuff. Two deep for sweaters or shirts is enough.

ACCESSORIES: HOW TO STORE

Belts: Belts can be hung, or rolled to store in a drawer or bin.

Boots and shoes:

1. If you have the space, have a shelf system built floor to ceiling within the closet. Vary shelf height according to the heel height of the shoes—less space for storing casual shoes, more space for high heels. If you invest in pull-out shelving, you'll have easy access to all pairs.

2. Or add a low shelf for shoe storage along the floor of the closet. Shoes will be tidy and accessible yet the closet floor can still be vacuumed.

3. Some people like to keep shoes in boxes. Store each pair in the box it came in, or transfer to a transparent shoe box. Label as to color and season: "Summer—navy flats."

4. Shoe racks are a perfectly acceptable storage system for shoes you wear regularly. (Keep less frequently worn pairs in boxes to guard against dust.)

   Don't use shoe bags. Grit from the shoes gathers in the pouches, and after a time the weight of the shoes causes the bag to sag and tear.

Handbags: These should stand on a shelf. Put seldom-used bags in cotton or linen sacks to minimize dust; stuff evening bags with tissue paper.

Silk scarves: Fold and store in a drawer or a shallow basket, or display on hooks or on a rack on the back of the closet door.

Socks: Roll or fold socks. Don't ball up pairs—it causes unnecessary stretching of the elastic.

Stockings: Stockings need to be labeled as to color, rolled, and stored carefully to avoid snags. Closet shops and mail-order companies sell stocking organizers that hang in a closet. Or you can use small plastic bags (one pair per bag) to minimize snags, and store them in a drawer or in a plastic box.

Ties: Hang a tie rack on the back of the closet door, or purchase one of the hanger-style tie racks.

Underwear: Roll underwear and store in an easily accessible drawer or plastic box.

JEWELRY

- Keep a small box or dish on the bureau for items you wear every day.

- The ideal storage system is a custom-made drawer. Make a blueprint of what you need by laying out all your jewelry in groups. Use drawer dividers (or have a carpenter create something permanent) to create the various sections of the drawer.

- Consider having a locksmith add a lock to this drawer. (Sometimes it's possible to install a side locking device so that it isn't obvious that the drawer has a lock.

- You can also use jewelry boxes—one for necklaces; one for pins; one for sets of jewelry that go together.

- Try the already-compartmentalized tackle and tool boxes for keeping other baubles, bangles, and beads sorted.

- Ask a jeweler about jewelry storage pouches that will keep silver from tarnishing.

- If you store jewelry in the original boxes or pouches, add labels so pieces are easy to locate.

- For specific types of pieces:

   —Earrings: Try storing pairs in ice trays. (The trays can be stacked and kept in a dresser drawer.) Or buy regular earring organizers.

   —Necklaces: Hang long ones from a necklace rack. They are easy to find and won't tangle. Those of value should be stored in a box, lying flat. If you no longer have the original box for a necklace with a very delicate chain, carefully wrap the chain around a thin strip of cardboard to prevent tangling. Store in a jewelry box or pouch.

   —Pins: Store in jewelry boxes or use a pincushion.

- Sort through your jewelry at least once a year so that you'll be reminded of the variety of pieces you have to wear.

LINEN CLOSETS

- Line linen-closet shelves with a quilted, scented, easy-to-clean vinyl fabric or paper.

- Keep only frequently used sheets and towels in the linen closet.

- Fold or roll towels in a uniform way and stack by color and by size.

- Sheets are best folded by set. Fold pillow case and fitted and flat sheet separately, then place the flat sheet and pillow case within the fitted sheet so they can be pulled out as a unit.

- When storing sheets, towels, or tablecloths, place on the shelf with the folded side out so that you can remove the number you need. (If the edges face out, it's hard to determine whether you have more than one.)

- Stack sheets according to family member (all sheets used on John's bed together, etc.); stack towels according to the bathroom in which they are used.

- If you lack storage in the bathroom, the linen closet is perfect for holding extra bathroom and medical supplies. Store in transparent bins or use a pull-out shelf or spinning caddy so that items are visible and accessible.

- Keep seldom-used blankets, quilts, and extra pillows in blanket and pillow covers.
- The floor of the linen closet should be used for large, bulky items or for smaller items stored in labeled bins or storage boxes.

H ALL CLOSETS

- If you have the luxury of two front hall closets, dedicate one to everyday coats, boots, and snowsuits. Use the other for dress coats and out-of-season coats in garment bags, and leave a spare foot or two to hang guests' coats.
- Do you have room to add shelving? Especially in an apartment where you're always looking for additional storage, it's worth putting in shelves even if you need a stepladder to get to them. (Store items you don't need regularly on difficult-to-reach shelves.)
- In some homes, the closet poles are higher than necessary. Consider whether lowering the pole and adding a more accessible shelf would make this closet more convenient. (Measure your longest coats to be sure they won't drag if the pole is lowered.)
- Coats should be hung on sturdy, well-designed hangers, and all should face the same direction.

- If each person has several coats, group them by family member.

- For adult scarves and gloves, purchase separate baskets or open bins to keep on the top shelf. When you need an item, you can take down the whole container, select what you need, and return the container to the shelf.

- Knit hats should be placed in a basket dedicated to soft hats.

- Hats with shapes should be kept in hatboxes or on a hat stand, or frequently worn ones can sit flat on shelves during the season in which they are used.

BACKDOORS
WHEN HOOKS ARE HANDY

Some families enter and leave the house most frequently through a rear entrance that leads to the garage or the most popular path to school. If so, that's where everyday coats, boots, hats, and gloves should go. (Use baskets or bins for gloves and headwear.) Hooks in a back hallway or mudroom work well, or try a coatrack near the most frequently used door. This also frees up space in your front hall closet.

- Install extra hooks for guest coats.
- Rainy climate? Dedicate a hook to slickers and keep umbrellas in a nearby umbrella stand.
- Keep items on hooks pared down. When fall turns to winter, remove and launder all light jackets, and hang them in a closet until they are needed in spring. When it's time to pull out the lightweight coats again, send the winter ones to the dry cleaners.
- Or purchase a tiered plastic-coated wire basket unit to place in your closet for storing outerwear accessories.
- Young children at home?
    - Hang hooks at child level so they can hang up their own coats.
    - Add a shoe bag to the back of the closet door and put hats and mittens in their own pouches.
- During winter, stand boots in a large shallow basket that is easy to pull out (for accessibility and so you can clean underneath).
- Is there room for a mirror on the back of the door? It's always great to be able to catch a peek at how you look before you run out the door.
- If all your outerwear storage is accommodated and you have closet space left over, use it for out-of-season accessories, holiday ornaments, etc.—anything you don't need access to regularly and which can be stores neatly.

5
HOME ENTERTAINING:
SMALL DINNER PARTIES AND OVERNIGHT GUESTS

WHAT'S AHEAD

Household Preparation
Mealtime Magic
Last-Minute Entertaining
Tips for Parents Who Entertain
The Overnight Guest: 23 Ways to Make a Stay Pleasant
If You Have a Separate Guest Bedroom
Helping Children Adjust

My oldest and dearest friend always has a smile on her face, except when she's entertaining. Countless times I've arrived for dinner, and there she is slaving over a hot stove—tired and grouchy; or she'll be popping out of a last-minute shower just as the guests arrive. She really does love dinner parties—so long as it's not at her house!

So if the words "Honey, the guests are here!" remind you of feeling dead-tired because you've worked so hard to get ready, then it's time to make some changes.

HOUSEHOLD PREPARATION FOR A SMALL DINNER PARTY

- Limit the number of projects you undertake in preparation for company. If you've been meaning to get the living room drapes cleaned anyway—and the dinner party gives you a deadline—then let that be the only major project you undertake.

- Plan where you will put coats. Check your hall closet. Be certain you have extra hangers and that the hanging space is adequate.

- Check the living room or deck as to conversation groupings. Is the furniture arranged in the best possible way?

- Tidy the rooms in which you'll be entertaining. The only important cleaning detail in a household is the bathroom. If it sparkles, guests will think the whole house does.

   —Wipe down sink and toilet bowl.

—Put out all fresh towels as well as guest towels. (Most guests will go to great lengths to avoid using the fancy guest towels, so it's important to have clean terry-cloth towels available as well.)

—Put out a fresh guest soap.

—Potpourri in winter or a small bouquet in summer can brighten this room and make it look as if you entertain all the time.

MEALTIME MAGIC

- Choosing to do a theme party can simplify the menu. A wintertime "picnic" lets you serve sandwiches and picnic food. A Western theme lends itself to burgers and beans; Mexican dishes can be easy to fix as well. And don't forget about potluck. Ask guests to bring a dish ready to serve or in an oven-to-table serving dish if it needs to be warmed.

- Unless you're a fabulous cook whose meals are almost always no-fail, select a few menus to perfect for company—a couple of great meals to grill in the summer; one or two warm selections for winter. Choose something for which the preparation is done in advance. Some wintertime soups and stews actually taste better the following day; and many chicken recipes can be prepared in the afternoon and all you need to do is bake it that night.

- When you select the menu, choose something that's easy to eat. If you're serving buffet and people will be eating on their laps, don't serve anything that must be cut.

- Work out logical side dishes that can also be prepared in advance. Few would suspect that homemade bread was actually made ten days ago and frozen; you can do the same with dessert cookies.

- Consider what local specialties you can add as a trademark. One family that lives near a fruit farm serves the farm's wonderful fruit pies (with ice cream) all summer long—entertaining made easy.

- Practice new recipes ahead of time, and note any adjustments you need to make.

- Note all ingredients for the dishes you plan to serve so that you can do your shopping in one trip. (Add club soda so that you'll have it on hand in case of mealtime spills.)

- What will you serve to drink? Take an inventory of your liquor, wine, beer, soda, and sparkling waters. Add lemons, limes, olives, and tomato and orange juice to your grocery list.

- Get out the dishes, serving platters, and serving utensils, and check to see that everything is in good condition (and not dusty, chipped, or tarnished).

- Some miscellaneous items to have on hand for easy entertaining include:

    —Bottle openers

    —Candles

- —Coasters
- —Cocktail napkins
- —Corkscrew
- —Garbage-can liners
- —Matches
- —Paper towels
- —Place cards (buy them or have your children create some)
- —Tablecloth (or mats) and napkins
- And on the day of the party have:
  - —Clean dish towels
  - —Extra ice (make or buy in advance)
- If you will be doing any mixing or cooking once guests have arrived, premeasure ingredients. Store them in small bowls or cups, refrigerate if necessary. Group them within the refrigerator.

- Set the table the night before or early in the day of the party.

- Fun centerpieces can often be found around the house. A grouping of children's colorful sculptures, vegetables in a basket, or a houseplant in bloom can work well.

- If you decide on flowers, order several days in advance and ask for an arrangement that is broad, not high, so people can talk over it. Arrange for delivery, or pick it up early on the day of your party.

- Prethink what needs to be done and write out a timetable so that once the evening is under way, you simply follow your written instructions to a flawless evening.

- Clear kitchen counters of everything but what is necessary.
- Empty kitchen trash, and start with a clean bag.
- Run and empty the dishwasher before the guests arrive so that you can load it as the evening progresses.
- Keep a list of who you've entertained, the date, what you've served, and any comments. It will make for easier entertaining the next time.

LAST-MINUTE ENTERTAINING

I was never so impressed with "entertaining magic" as on the day several years ago when a friend invited us over for a last-minute Sunday lunch. The meal was spectacular, the table beautifully set. How was she able to feed six adults and three children with such ease and style with only two hours' notice?

The secret is in a do-it-ahead, have-it-on-hand system:

1. Always have on hand some foods or sauces that have been prepared ahead of time. (Remember to cook double and freeze half.) Special foods that freeze well include:

   —Pesto or tomato sauces

   —Soups

—Quiche, pot roast, even lasagna

—Uncooked chicken cutlets and fish fillets (freeze well and are easy to prepare)

A microwave will help you thaw these items faster.

2. Purchase certain staples that are easy to work with:

   —Frozen pie crusts

   —Bread or biscuit mix

   —Canned tomatoes and tomato paste

3. Stock up on fresh salad greens and seasonal fruit.

4. Keep on hand homemade salad dressing.

5. Add a bottle of wine and your meal is complete.

6. Invest in a good supply of cloth napkins so that clean ones are always available.

• Remember that practice makes perfect. The more you do it, the easier it becomes.

THE OVERNIGHT GUEST: 23 Ways to Make a Stay Pleasant

Whether the guest is sleeping on a pull-out couch in a den or borrowing your child's bedroom for a night, here are some thoughtful touches to provide:

TIPS FOR PARENTS

- Let your children help by making place cards and place mats.

- Ask older children to help take coats and clear dishes.

- If this is a dinner for adults only, explain that to your children and provide a sitter or plan special activities for them.

- If children will be among your guests, consider having the other family over for lunch or an early dinner.

- One big table or an adult table and a children's table? Babies need to be with parents; older kids generally love having a table of their own. If you have a child-size table, the nursery-school set will particularly enjoy sitting there if it's accessorized with a bouquet and pretty napkins.

—Alarm clock that has a luminous dial (overnight guests or those who have traveled from a different time zone may be awake at odd hours)

—Flashlight if they need to get up in the night

—Water glass

—One or two extra blankets (you can't judge how guests will view the temperature of your house)

WHO ENTERTAIN

- When children will be joining you, show your own child where everyone will sit at dinner to avoid a big scene if a guest sits in "his chair."

- If four or more young ones are invited, hire a neighborhood teen to come and take charge.

- Plan activities for your children and the guest children—they may not have a lot in common. Renting videotapes is a good investment, and depending on their ages, you may want to set up a spot for them to do art work or play games.

- When young guests arrive, identify the parts of the house and yard where the children will play, and tell them where the adults will be.

- Plan food that will please the children. If the adults are eating something exotic, you may want to have pasta, sandwiches, or pizza on hand.

—Two pillows (many people use an extra pillow for reading in bed)

—Luggage rack (buy one that folds up to be stored in the closet until the next guest arrives)

—Clothes tree if there is no convenient closet for a guest to use; extra hangers if there is a closet in the room

- Provide a small dish to hold coins, rings, or other jewelry.

- Give the guest a set of towels and a washcloth that are set aside for "guests only."

- Collect small bottles of shampoos, lotions, and creams, and put them in a small basket in the guest quarters. Or provide regular-sized ones in the bathroom. If a guest has forgotten something, it's nice to have it available without having to ask.

- Fresh flowers provide a welcoming touch.

- A "Do Not Disturb" sign can help a guest establish "visiting" hours. An elderly relative might appreciate the opportunity to nap undisturbed, while still being able to have the "welcome" mat out to the children most of the time.

- A guest who will be with you for more than one night might appreciate:

   —Extra key so they needn't disturb you when coming and going

   —Photocopy of local street map showing your neighborhood so that they can walk without getting lost

   —List of suggested walks to take or local stores to visit

   —Laundry hamper with a note as to the day you wash

IF YOU HAVE A SEPARATE GUEST BEDROOM

- Sleep overnight in the room yourself so that you can evaluate what will make the room more comfortable.
- Arrange furniture so there is a small table beside the bed.
- Provide a bedside lamp (two if it's a double bed) so that guests can easily read in bed and so that they can get into bed safely before turning out the last light.
- Leave the top two drawers empty in a guest-room bureau so that guests who are staying a few days can unpack.
- Keep a radio or small television in the room.
- Have on hand an interesting selection of books or magazines.

(Watch out—they may not want to leave!)

HELPING YOUR CHILD ADJUST TO OVERNIGHT GUEST

- If the guest will be sleeping in the child's room, explain why this is necessary and let the child help prepare the room

- If young guests are coming, too, let your child select a few toys that he or she needn't share.

- Explain to him or her any changes in schedule for the next few days.

- A house guest disrupts the family rhythm, and you may be happily chatting with the guest at just the moment your child hoped to catch you alone in the kitchen. Establish a signal so that either of you can notify the other that it's time to talk privately for a moment.

6
HOUSEHOLD FILES

WHAT'S AHEAD

File Cabinets and More
What to File
Creating a System
How to File
Ten Filing Rules
Tickler Files
Filing Day-to-Day Financial Information

Paper is a No. 1 American problem. More and more accumulates every day, so unless you develop a useful filing system you'll never be able to find what you're looking for. And if you can't find it when you need it, then your system isn't working for you.

In general, I see three types of problems with filing:

Client A has difficulty throwing anything away, and when he or she files, it's for posterity. These homes generally have papers **everywhere**.

Client B has a filing system, but it doesn't work: "I know I filed the warranty on my new camera. I just can't figure out where."

Client C just can't cope. The mail arrives; the children bring home school papers; information is brought in from the office. . . . It's always the same: overwhelming! Nothing is sorted or filed . . . the family can't find a thing.

If any of this sounds familiar, keep reading.

FILE CABINETS AND MORE

Any home needs a good place to put papers. Consider:

File cabinet: Most homes should have a filing cabinet—two- or four-drawer, depending on your needs. A good file cabinet should last a lifetime, so start out with the best you can find. (Second-hand or lesser quality is fine for the basement, but your main file cabinet should be first-rate.) Look for:

- **The appropriate size.** Two drawers? Four drawers? Drawers long enough for legal-size files or regular size (81/2 by 11)? If you're an attorney or do work that involves many legal documents, the legal-size drawers will better suit your needs.

- **A unit that uses a suspension filing system** ("hanging" files hold regular file folders). Filing and retrieval are simplified, and the hanging files prevent the domino effect within a drawer.

- **Vertical** or **lateral files**, depending on your space. Most people find that vertical file cabinets (conventional file cabinets, in which the files are stored front to back in each drawer) are easiest to find space for in most homes. But if you're setting up a home office, take a look at lateral files. The drawers are wider than they are deep, and the files run from side to side within the cabinet, giving you easy access to the full row of files. This style is very convenient, if it can be accommodated in the space you have planned.

Where should you put your "active" file cabinet? Never in the basement or attic. Put the cabinet in a central location. Is there room in the kitchen? Do you have a home office? You might even hide it in a closet. ("Inactive" files can be stored in file boxes or old file cabinets that are out of the way.)

Or combine two functions. Stretch a board across two double-drawer file cabinets to create quite a serviceable work space.

Metal file box: If you're young and single, you may find that a simple file box is adequate for your needs. Available in a couple of sizes, these boxes can store official paper neatly and are perfectly serviceable if you are diligent about throwing out or have not yet accumulated much.

Rolling file cart: Some of these look terrific—a white mesh cart with colored files makes for a snazzy and convenient way to keep your files. While I prefer a closed cabinet, where dust can't gather, I agree that these rolling carts provide a great mobile office.

WHAT TO FILE

Most households need files for the following information:

Bank: Account numbers and information, bank officers and telephone numbers, loan information, etc. (The final section of this chapter addresses how to file day-to-day financial information.)

Car: Owner's manual, payment book, sales and maintenance records.

Correspondence: Business correspondence, such as documentation of a letter of complaint; personal correspondence including letters from friends and relatives. Some people need two separate files.

Church or synagogue: Service schedules and information about volunteer commitments.

Credit-card information: A record of the charge cards you have, their numbers, the credit agreement, and the telephone numbers to call in case of loss or theft. (Or you can register with a credit-card service bureau. For a fee they keep a record of your cards, and in case of loss or theft, they do the notifying.) Also keep infrequently used credit cards here.

Education records: Official records, report cards, test scores, pertinent letters, and other related material. Establish a separate file for each family member.

Holidays: Ideas for next year, your holiday card list, record of annual monetary gifts, the size of Christmas tree, etc.

Housing information: A copy of your lease, if you rent; if you own, home-improvement information, closing and selling costs, copies of contracts, etc.

Job-related information: Employee-benefit information, pension records, and other miscellaneous information pertaining to your work.

Important documents: Copies of birth certificates, passports, marriage license, divorce papers, wills, letter of last instructions (originals should be kept in a safe-deposit box), and notes on the location of any other important papers, as well as name and telephone number of accountant, lawyer, broker, etc. Also keep on file social security and driver's license number.

Insurance: Copies of all policies as well as a list of policy numbers, names of the insured, issuing company, agent, type and amount of coverage, for an at-a-glance review. A copy of your personal-property inventory (a list and photos of your household possessions and any insured item of particular worth) should be kept here, though the original should be kept in your safe-deposit box.

Investment information: Investment records, along with brokerage statements and transaction slips.

Magazine subscriptions: A record of magazines and renewal dates so you'll know when you really need to resubscribe.

Medical records for each family member: Dates of relevant immunizations, copies of school or camp physicals, notes about personal health problems, etc. Each family member should have a separate file.

Membership information: Cards and information regarding clubs, museums, zoological societies, and any other types of organizations to which you belong.

Retirement: Information on your IRA or Keogh plan, or brochures on a retirement community. If you have both types of information, create two "Retirement" file subcategories.

Tax information: Copies of previous years' returns, and notes for the upcoming year.

Warranties: Warranties and service agreements on all your appliances and equipment.

In addition to these basics, keep files for the following, when appropriate:

Entertaining: A list of whom you've entertained, when, and what you served.

Financial planning: Articles or information about saving for college or retirement—whatever your financial goals are.

Gift lists: A record of holiday and birthday presents to provide an easy way to check what you've given in years past. Place here, or file the gift list with your holiday information.

Health: Articles on migraines, back pain, nutrition, etc.

Hobbies: Gardening? Furniture refinishing? A new hobby you're considering? If you have many interests, you may want separate files.

New pursuits: Considering switching jobs? Thinking of going back to school? Open up a file and name it appropriately.

Pets: Pedigree papers, medical and vaccination records, as well as the names of dog trainers, walkers, or kennels.

Restaurants: Reviews of local restaurants, names of caterers, etc.

Shopping and bargains: Names of local stores recommended by friends, ads that attract you, discount coupons for local businesses.

Travel: Articles on locations of interest to plan your next vacation.

Volunteer-related information: Are you running a big fundraiser for the school? Start a file on it. If it's a major project, create several files by breaking the material down into subcategories.

CREATING A SYSTEM

Create a system that makes it easy for you and other family members to find the information you need.

- A combination of alphabetizing files and color-coding the labels is foolproof. (I like to color-code both label and files.) When you open the drawer, you'll know that the "Financial Planning" file is halfway back in the drawer, and that it's green. Given the categories above, choose a color for:

  —Financial information—files pertaining to your bank, credit cards, investment files, and related information would all be the same color

  —Each family member—include medical, education files, etc. (If you color-code towels and toothbrushes, too, use the same color for each person here.)

  —General files (all else)

- Set up other color categories as needed. If you have three or more files for your PTA work, then you're ready to assign a special color to the PTA.

- If your file system uses more than four colors, make a color key for the front of your file cabinet to help others who might be looking for something. (List the name of each family member and the color for each, as well as the special categories to which you've assigned a color.)

- Along with the color key, provide family members with an index of key topics and the way in which you filed them. Store this list in the front of the first drawer of the file cabinet. Your spouse may be looking for information about the car under "Car," while you filed it under "Automobile." School records might be under "Education"; party ideas might be filed under "Entertaining." You need to create a way for others to be able to use your system.

HOW TO FILE:

- Buy:

    —New file folders (don't start a new system with beat-up old files left over from college)

    —Hanging files to hold the file folders, if your drawer or file system requires them

    —Labels (in several colors)

- You'll also need:

    —Pen

    —Boxes (for holding the papers until you break them into categories for files)

• Set aside time for this project. You'll need a couple of hours for your first session. Once you've got a system, you'll be able to work in ten- or fifteen-minute blocks of time.

• Choose a place to work where you can spread out. If you're filing for the first time, it will be easier to work on the floor and lay everything flat at the beginning.

• Gather papers to be filed from all over the house and bring them into one room.

• Boxes should be labeled by general category. A "Financial Information" box may actually be broken down into four or five files, but you need to gather everything together before you know exactly what those subcategories will be.

• If you know the file categories you'll use, label file folder labels with appropriate names. These papers will go directly into the files.

• Take the stack of papers to be filed under your new system, and go through them one by one.

• For each piece of paper ask:

—"Will I ever need this again? If I do, is there another easy way to get it?" For example, a recent newspaper article about ski vacations might be easily available at the library or on the on-line computer service to which you subscribe, thereby freeing you from keeping an article "just in case."

—"Does it add anything new to information I already have on this topic?" Don't save articles, brochures, or booklets that repeat basic information that you already have on file.

—"When and how will I want to retrieve this?" If you're going to Vermont next summer, then an article about a folk-art museum you'd like to visit should go in a "Vermont" file—a subcategory of your "Travel" file, not in a file about folk art. (After you visit, you may choose to refile the article in your "Folk Art" file.)

• Put aside papers you can't categorize. By the end, you may find that several items fall into a logical grouping.

• Whether you can finish in one session or whether it takes several, just keep working until you have everything filed. From then on you need only maintain the files.

TEN FILING RULES

1. Write the date and source of the material on every paper to be filed.

2. File regularly. Some people file a piece of paper as they finish with it. (It's the fastest way to get it done.) Others may want "To File" baskets on their desks to collect items. Before putting an item in the basket, label the file in which it will eventually be placed. (This keeps you from having to reread or reevaluate when

you file.) If there is a date at which you'll no longer need the information, make a "Destroy after (date)" notation to make it easier to clean the file in the future. Be sure to set aside time, perhaps on the weekend, to take care of all filing.

3. If you're starting a new project, create a file folder for it. This is far more efficient than stacking the information somewhere around the house.

4. If a piece of paper would be appropriate in two separate files, photo-copy the item and put it in both files, or place a cross-referencing note in one file and the article in the other file.

5. All filed articles or documents should be complete. If you are filing two articles from a magazine, and article A is on the front of one page and article B is on the back of the same page, photocopy the pages so that each is whole when filed.

6. Staple relevant material together. Paper clips tend to catch on other papers within the file.

7. Organize within the file. If dates are particularly relevant, order chronologically. If there are several names included in one file, then organize alphabetically.

8. If you have to take something out of a file for any length of time, leave a note, specifying the item's whereabouts. Perhaps you need an opinion on your insurance policy and decide to show it to someone. Write where the copy of the policy is so that you don't forget.

9. Weed out regularly. Whenever you pull a file to retrieve a paper, take a few minutes to clean out the file. Toss what is no longer relevant to keep your files pared down. On the inside of the file folder, note the date on which you last sorted through it. That way you'll know at a glance if you haven't been through a file in a very long time.

10. If you're no longer referring to certain files, evaluate whether the information within can be refiled more appropriately or can be tossed. If neither option is appropriate, move the file to an "inactive" status. Use a portable file box or a cardboard box to hold "inactive" files (worth keeping, but do not need to be accessible). Store in closet, basement, or attic.

TICKLER FILES

Many people don't like to file pending papers—papers they're going to use or act on in the next few days. I've seen enough refrigerator doors covered to overflowing and enough bulletin boards with yellowing schedules to say with great certainty you **must** file these papers. The secret lies in creating "Tickler" files.

• Take thirteen file folders, and select a color for this group of files—one that will identify these as your "Tickler" files. (This is a slightly simpler system than the one recommended for use in an office.)

- Label the folder for each month, with one labeled "This Week."

- These are your "action" files. On December 20, you receive an invitation for a party in January. A map and directions are enclosed. RSVP and write the date on your calendar; toss the invitation and file the map and directions in your January file.

- You need to follow up with your insurance company on a matter they swore would be resolved in two months; file this reminder and related information two months hence.

- Your son needs to go back to the ophthalmologist in four months; file the doctor's business card accordingly.

- The file labeled "This Week" holds all the items you will need this week. The receipt for your VCR that's being repaired, the card reminding you to change your dental appointment, the tickets you need for the opera on Saturday.

FILING DAY-TO-DAY FINANCIAL INFORMATION

Financial information falls into three categories:

1. Documents that are so valuable that they must be kept in a safe-deposit box. In addition to legal documents, this includes information such as stock certificates, titles to property, trust documents, information regarding pension plans, mortgage papers. All should be stored in a safe-deposit box.

2. Information to file for retrieval over the years. This would pertain to advisory information, general financial information, etc. This material all belongs in the "active" filing system described above.

3. Day-to-day financial information that is maintained for family financial management and backing up tax filings—this would include all bills, payment records, bank statements, and receipts, as well as canceled checks.

For canceled checks: Purchase a canceled-checks file folder for the year. Checks should be filed by month. Label the folder clearly with the year and the account number:

"200_ Jane Jones
Banker's Bank, Acct #___"

To file the day-to-day bills and information:

• Buy a Household Affairs file—available at most stationery stores. Some are set up by month; others are categorized: Automobile, Bank Records, Income Taxes, Insurance Records, Medical/Dental, Real-Estate Taxes, Receipts, Rent and Mortgage Records, Utilities, etc. Label this file with the year.

• As you accumulate them, charge slips should be stored in a small envelope marked "Charge Slips—July," for example. The envelope itself can be stored in the "Receipts" section of the Household Affairs file. (When the bill comes in, match the slips against the invoices before paying.)

• As you receive invoices, file them in an "Unpaid Bills" section, chronologically by due date. Set up a routine for paying them twice a month. By paying bills every other week instead of once a month, you can pay closer to the date that the money is due, and yet you'll find that you'll never incur a finance charge because the payment is made on time.

• Throughout the year, file all receipts and paid bills by month or under specific categories, whichever you prefer.

• At the end of the year, simply fold up the file and put it in a safe place in case you ever need to document anything or if your tax files are ever called into question. (Tax-related records should be kept for six years.)

• In December, buy and label new folders for the approaching year.

7

THE HOUSEHOLD NOTEBOOK

WHAT'S AHEAD

To Create Your Notebook
What Goes Inside
Trimming Down

Every household needs a simple way to keep track of household projects and miscellaneous information. (See Chapter 6, Household Files, for tips on filing other materials.) The notebook is part planner and part guidebook, to keep the household running smoothly even when you aren't there.

TO CREATE YOUR NOTEBOOK

- To set up, you'll need:
  —Looseleaf notebook (nine by twelve)
  —Dividers with pockets, perhaps as many as ten or twelve of them (the divider pockets can hold cleaning tickets, business cards, and other miscellaneous information)
  —Paper
- Keep your Household Notebook in a central location, such as the kitchen.

WHAT GOES INSIDE

Your Household Notebook categories might include:

How-to-operate information: Keep instruction booklets inside a divider pocket, and if you ever expect anyone else (house sitter, housekeeper, visiting relative) to operate anything, from the washer to the VCR, add simple instructions written by you. For example, the information on running the washing machine should include personal preferences, such as the temperature settings you use as well as the basics about how to turn it on. The VCR information might include a diagram and/or written instructions so that a babysitter or grandparent can put on a tape for your toddler.

"What to do if . . ." information: What do you do if a circuit breaker trips? What if the washing machine overflows? What if the car won't start? By assembling important telephone numbers (plumber, electrician, etc.), together with "insider" information (which rooms in the house are on which electrical circuits), you can be prepared for many emergencies whether you're home or not.

Household maintenance schedule: Here's the best place to keep track of information such as when the gutters were last cleaned or when the boiler was checked. If you're thinking of putting in a new hot-water heater, clip ads and articles and put in a divider pocket, along with notes on what the experts tell you about what your household needs.

Car pools: Car-pooling responsibilities should be noted on the Family Calendar, but if you need to swap with someone, you could check the full car-pool schedule, which should be neatly filed in your Household Notebook.

School notices that you need to refer to within a week or so. You don't need them long enough to file them, so clip them into a section here, and you'll know what your child needs for the field trip next week. (Note relevant dates on the Family Calendar.)

Special plans: Thinking of taking a trip? Use this space for your first list of things to do before you leave. Also note the instructions you'll want to remember to give the sitter before you go away.

Special projects: If a special project requires more than two or three steps, then it deserves a section of this notebook—or a notebook of its own. This is the perfect way to stay on top of any complex household project that requires tracking down lots of details. The system permits you to work through your plans on paper, keep track of details, and have an important record of relevant information to carry with you. Here are examples:

Thinking of selling your home? In your Notebook, create a section for related information. One page would list the realtors with whom you've spoken, their telephone numbers, and any comments they had. The next page might hold advertisements (clipped or stapled to the page) for comparable houses, with their prices, etc.

Or suppose you need to get the roof repaired. If you're getting bids from several people, this is the place to record names and numbers. Staple business cards to the page, or slip them into the appropriate divider pocket. When a special project, such as the roof repair, is completed, the information should be removed from your Notebook. If you liked the roofer, his business card (and those of any others whom you would let bid on a job again) should be filed in a long-term "Household" file. (See Chapter 6, Household Files.)

Redecorating? For just one room, you would note down room and furniture dimensions, and in the divider pocket keep items such as paint chips and wallpaper and fabric samples you're considering. Telephone numbers of craftsmen and fabric and furniture or supply stores should also be recorded here. Should you be doing the entire house, you would be best served by selecting a portable notebook dedicated to the project. That way you can keep all the information together in one easy-to-carry collection.

TRIMMING DOWN

At least once a year—January is a good time—you should go through your Household Notebook and weed out information that you no longer need. This is also a good time to set up new categories for projects for the upcoming year.

8

THE KITCHEN: CREATING AN ORGANIZED SPACE

WHAT'S AHEAD

Space Assessment

Weeding Out

"I Need More Counter Space!"

General Storage

Kitchen Extras

Food Storage

Refrigerator

In most homes, the kitchen is not only the food-preparation area but also the household command center and a favorite spot for eating, talking on the telephone, and, sometimes, watching television. In order to fulfill all these functions, the kitchen needs to be well organized:

—The room needs to accommodate all of the family's needs.

—There must be defined work centers.

—Small appliances and dishes should be stored near where they are used.

—Counters must be kept clear in order for you to work.

SPACE ASSESSMENT

Begin by reevaluating the use of your kitchen, so that you can better utilize the space you have. If you intend to redesign, the conclusions you reach will be helpful to the person who is drawing up the plans.

• What purposes does your kitchen currently serve? Is it a food-service room only, or must it accommodate schoolchildren doing homework, or teens fixing snacks and talking on the phone?

• Write down what you ideally want from your kitchen. An eating area? A mini-office? A better area for baking? More storage? A more convenient location for recyclables?

- Also note any complaints you have about the way the kitchen is currently arranged.

- Next, identify the work centers that are important to you. Most kitchens need:

  —A food preparation and cooking area

  —Space around the sink for washing fruits and vegetables and rinsing dishes

  —A baking area

  —A serving area

If you prepare many dishes from scratch, then creating a perfect work center for cooking will take priority; if you bake a lot, then you may want to set up a terrific baking area. Your kitchen should be arranged so that it works the best for **you**.

- As you evaluate your current space and storage, try this test for any item used frequently: Can you get it out in one simple motion? If you have to unstack several pots to get to the one you use most often, or if you have to feel around in the silverware drawer for the oversized spoon you use for cooking, then you need to reevaluate your current storage system.

  - Also consider whether your lighting and electrical outlets are adequate. Better lighting can improve kitchen working conditions, and a more convenient outlet can simplify many jobs.

WEEDING OUT

I'm going to reveal a well-kept kitchen secret:

**You have the right to toss things out
or pass them on to others if you don't use them!**

Limit what you store, and kitchen space automatically frees up. Use the following guidelines in weeding out:

1. If you don't use it, don't store it. Items such as fondue pots and woks are enormous fun if you still enjoy preparing meals with them, but if your interest has waned, make room for other things.

2. If you use it infrequently and your kitchen is crowded, store it elsewhere in the house. Large serving pieces or articles used seasonally, such as picnic supplies, should be boxed and labeled. Store on a shelf in the attic, basement, garage, apartment storage bin, or even on a high shelf in a closet.

3. Consider whether you need duplicates. If you cook a great deal, you probably do need several saucepans, but do you really need three sets of casserole dishes? Or how about those old muffin tins you bought at a yard sale? Now that you have some of the no-stick variety, you really don't need to keep the old ones.

"I NEED MORE COUNTER SPACE!"

When I tour a kitchen, I often see a cookie jar, a microwave, a toaster oven, a mixer, a blender, a coffee maker, a draining rack, canisters, a basket with hot pads, detergent, sponges, and a television all lined up neatly (or not so neatly) along the counter. The people these kitchens belong to don't need more counter space. They need to better utilize what they have.

- The only items that belong on the counter are those that are used **at least** once a day.

- All else should be put away. Make room in a cupboard for the mixer and blender; put cookie jars and sugar and flour canisters on a cupboard shelf.

- Store only three or four favorite cookbooks in the kitchen, and move the rest to another room, where you have more space.

- Visit an appliance store and consider which of your counter-top appliances could be top-mounted. Can openers, toaster ovens, and some of the smaller microwave ovens can all be mounted beneath a cupboard, freeing some of the counter space below. If you should be buying a new stove, consider one that has the oven below and microwave above.

- If an item must be out (not in a cupboard), consider this alternative: Have a narrow shelf added between the counter and upper cupboard for small appliances and other items, such as a few cookbooks, frequently used spices, and a coffee maker.

- If you're still short on work space, there are alternatives:

  —A rolling cart with a butcher-block top can provide storage underneath and a work surface on top. Roll it out of the way when you're finished.

  —At the end of one counter, have a flip-up counter top added. Put it up while you're working; fold it down when you've finished.

  —A cutting board that fits over the sink often extends work space with a minimum of effort. It provides for tidy cleanup as you work, since you can push the excess directly into the sink or the disposal. And since you are cutting over sink space, it leaves the counter free for other preparations.

  —If you have a large kitchen with space for a center island, have one built. It provides an extra work station for a spouse or for children, and if it's designed with cupboards or bookshelves beneath, it greatly increases your storage space.

GENERAL STORAGE

Items used together should be stored together, and they should be stored near where they are used. Everyday dishes should be stored near the sink or dishwasher (for convenience in putting away); open boxes of cereal should be stored near your meal-preparation area; most frequently used pots and pans should be hung or stored near the stove. A baking center should have mixer, bowls, measuring cups, and spoons nearby, as well as basic ingredients: flour, sugars, vanilla, baking soda and powder.

WORTH THE TIME

Cupboards:

—Hang stemware by its base from a rack that attaches to a cupboard shelf bottom. (Choose an upper cupboard for this type of storage.)

—Spinning caddies and stairstepped rack systems can help make items stored in the back of cupboards more accessible.

—Adjustable shelves in cupboards are helpful in creating customized storage. Or try plastic-coated wire shelf racks. Plates or bowls can fit underneath, and another item can be stored on top.

—Add sliding shelves. They increase accessibility, particularly in lower cupboards, where you're likely to be storing large pots and pans and baking supplies.

—Cutting boards, cookie sheets, and trays should all be stored vertically to take less space. If you have a narrow cabinet, per haps by the oven or the refrigerator, have a carpenter fit it with a divider or two.

—If you have an odd nook—perhaps a six-inch space between counter and refrigerator—have a slide-out food-storage unit built to hold certain canned goods.

Inside the cupboard door:

Visit a kitchen shop or hardware store and look for inside and on-the-door organizers to hold the following:

—boxes of foil, plastic bags and wrap

—pot lids

—garbage (If you don't have a garbage disposal, install a small garbage holder inside the cupboard under the sink.) Before purchasing, be certain you have the clearance you need for in stalling these items.

Drawers:

—Use dividers. Silverware organizers are easily available, as are divider kits, which help you create the drawer divisions that are right for you. Even kitchen drawers filled with miscellaneous utensils will be manageable if there is separation of space.

—If you prefer not to store boxes of waxed paper, plastic wrap, and foil on the back of a cupboard door, consider putting them in a drawer. Add a small container to hold twist ties so they don't get lost within the drawer.

—Small drawers can become spice drawers. Use dividers to des ignate a compartment within the drawer, and then label the top of the spice lids so that they can be read at a glance.

Storage on display:

—Decorative hooks or ceiling racks can provide storage for cook ware with handles—the more attractive the pot, the more at tractive the storage system.

—Accordion-style racks that pull out from the wall provide for pot storage by nesting one within the other.

—On-the-wall storage using a peg board or magnetic strip can be handy for knives (in a household with no young children), mea suring spoons, or small pots and pans.

—Open metal shelving from a commercial supply house can make for interesting and functional storage.

—Colored plastic stacking bins on a cart can be attractive and extend your storage space.

Storage within storage:

—To stack or not to stack?

Do stack storage containers that aren't used daily.

Do stack plates and bowls.

Don't stack when you use the largest of the set daily (frying pan?), because then you're continually unstacking; try to give it a place of its own.

Keep all stacks low.

—Use large containers to collect groups of smaller items. A plastic box (no lid) can be kept under the sink to hold sponges, scouring pad, and dish scrubber. When storing extra plastic food-storage containers, use one larger container to hold lids of smaller ones.

—To keep track of what plastic top fits what container bottom, take a marking pen and write a corresponding number on each.

KITCHEN EXTRAS

• Need a kitchen office? Is there space for a small counter or desk? A bulletin board above, bookshelves and phone nearby, and a place for the Family Calendar can give you a highly functional command center. In a drawer or organizer, store tape, paper clips, pads, and pens. If you have room, add a small standing file.

• If you find that many of your cupboards are difficult to reach, purchase a decorative stool or an arm extender.

• If you're remodeling your kitchen, look for all the added conveniences that are being built into new cabinetry and appliances. Some sink cabinets now have a front panel that tilts down to hold sponges, soap, and scrub brushes; pull-out counters and cutting boards are being added to both cabinets and appliances. Investigate what will work for you.

• The kitchens of today need space for trash to be recycled. Most items need to be rinsed, so storage near the sink is ideal. What you choose as the receptacle largely depends on how your community wants items sorted:

—No sorting necessary? Use a single undersink container.

—Sorting required? Under-sink storage of several containers can be cumbersome. Hardware stores sell trash-can dividers so that you can create separation within a single trash can. Or stackable bins might be an answer.

—Some families set up garage or basement storage instead of making room in the kitchen. Rinse and drain the items, and take them to the receptacles daily at the same time you run your dishwasher, so that it becomes a regular habit.

• If your community does not yet have curbside pickup for recyclables, be certain any storage container you buy fits easily into the trunk of your car to make trips to the town dump as simple as possible.

FOOD STORAGE

Whether it's one oversized cupboard or a closet you can convert into a pantry, everyone needs a place to store food. Packages of baking ingredients and open food containers used regularly, such as breakfast cereal, should be stored in the main part of the kitchen. Other foods—extra peanut butter and pasta, canned goods, unopened sauces, etc.—that don't require refrigeration belong in a pantry.

• A walk-in pantry is ideal. Is there a closet in the kitchen (or vicinity), or could a carpenter create a pantry from a nook in the kitchen?

• Pantry shelving should be custom-built in graduated depths to accommodate everything from the tiniest cans, such as tomato paste, and extra spices to large bulky goods. Items are highly visible, and shelf space is not wasted. Shelves should be finished in a high-gloss paint or polyurethane for quick and easy wipe-downs.

• Group all food by type (soups, canned fruit, pasta, backup supplies of items such as flour and sugar).

• Label shelves as to what belongs where so that other family members can help put items away.

WORTH THE TIME

• Alphabetize large groups of foods, such as soups or spices.

• In cupboards or pantry, spinning caddies come in handy for all sorts and sizes of things, because they prevent items from being lost in the back.

- Use a soda can dispenser (available in catalogs and kitchen and hardware stores) to hold canned goods such as soups.

- Once you open a box of anything (crackers, pasta, cookies), put the food in a see-through container. It's visible and will stay fresh.

- Potatoes and onions and other root vegetables can be stored in wire or mesh baskets in a lower cupboard or on the bottom shelf of the pantry.

- Wine should be stored horizontally on a slotted shelf.

- The place where you store food should be dark and dry. Keep the door closed as much as possible to keep light from coming in.

THE REFRIGERATOR

- Designate specific shelves for certain items. While the location of juice and milk containers may be obvious, the fresh fruit, the margarine, and the children's lunches can all have a designated space where they belong. It makes food easier to find, and it simplifies taking inventory.

- Items used most frequently should be stored near the front of the shelves, less frequently used items toward the back.

• Group foods together by category or use. (Fresh vegetables belong near one another, but it's also handy to group all lunch-making ingredients.)

• Date and label baked goods and leftovers, particularly those you freeze.

• Consider a spinning caddy for the refrigerator to best utilize space in the back.

• Use soda can dispensers to hold refrigerated soda.

• Don't waste door space. Group what you store there—salad dressings; condiments, etc.

• If you have a separate freezer for long-term storage, set up an inventory system. When you purchase or have delivered certain items, note down what you have. Keeping track after that is easy, because all that is entailed is marking off what you use:

Bread, whole wheat	~~4~~	3	
Bread, rye	6		
Chicken parts	3 pkgs.		
Chicken, whole	2		
Ground beef	~~5~~	~~4~~	3
Salmon	4		
Steaks	2		
Trout	~~8~~	7	

9
THE LAUNDRY

WHAT'S AHEAD

Location, Location, Location
The Family Laundry Center
Laundry Supplies
Ironing Equipment
Laundry Schedule
Before You Wash
Folding and Putting Away
Using a Laundromat
or Community Laundry Center

When it comes to laundry, most people wish they could avoid it; some have no idea what they are doing and ruin it. Others resort to hiring someone else to tackle "ring around the collar." Letting it pile up is a solution for some, like the young man who would collect several weeks' worth of laundry to take home to mother—who lived several hundred miles away.

Washday is no picnic, but there is a way to make doing the laundry just a small part of your day. The key to doing the laundry quickly and easily is a well-organized laundry center and an unvarying schedule for getting it done. If you use a laundromat or community laundry center, skip to "Laundry Supplies" and read on from there.

LOCATION, LOCATION, LOCATION

If you have the good fortune to be renovating or building a new home, establish a separate room or area for the laundry. The following locations offer advantages and disadvantages:

- **Near the bedrooms:** This is ideal. It's convenient for tossing in a load of laundry and getting it moved to the dryer, and you'll no longer need to lug heavy baskets up and down stairs.

- **In or near the kitchen:** This location is convenient for managing the wash. However, it may require that kitchen projects be put away before starting a load of laundry. Keep in mind that the machinery is noisy, and it's best not to run a washer or dryer during meals.

- **In the basement:** A laundry center in the basement offers plenty of space. Tile or indoor-outdoor carpeting, a good paint job, and some pictures on the wall can make it a cheerful place to work.

THE FAMILY LAUNDRY CENTER

A well-planned laundry room should have:

- Washer and dryer. If you're short on space, select a front-loading washer and dryer so that you'll have the top surface of the machines for folding and stacking.

- Separate sink for hand laundry. It's nice not to have to scour the kitchen sink in order to handwash the baby's sweater.

- Flat surface for sorting and folding clean clothing. Select a sturdy table, or have a counter built in the laundry room. If you should renovate your kitchen, retire the old cabinets to the laundry area for extra storage and a folding surface.

- Medium-sized shelf or closed cabinet near the washer to hold supplies.

- Drying rack.

- Pole for hanging; supply of hangers.

- Five or more labeled laundry baskets:

  —Three medium to large baskets: one for light, one for dark, and one for colored washes.

  —One small basket to hold any laundry that requires special handling.

  —A small basket to hold laundry for each bedroom. Clean laundry is placed in the basket, and the basket can be taken directly to the proper room.

- Widely spaced shelving along one wall can provide convenient storage for the various baskets. If there's no room for shelving, buy baskets that stack.
- Wastebasket.

LAUNDRY SUPPLIES

On the shelf or cabinet by the washer keep:

- Laundry detergent (if your detergent does not come with a built-in measuring cup, buy one and keep it on the shelf near the washer)
- Prewash product
- Cleaning fluid
- Bleach
- Bars of soap
- Fabric softener

In addition, you'll want:

- Rubber gloves

- Mesh bags that zip or tie shut for washing socks and/ or lingerie and other small items

- A small box or canister for the forgotten treasures found in the pockets of dirty jeans

- Small container of safety pins

- Small sewing kit (needle, spools of white and black thread, scissors) so that you can mend small holes or trim loose threads before putting the item in the washer

- Reference book on stain removal

- Index-card box to file special washing instructions (Have divider cards with each family member's name on it and file by owner's name. When you need to launder your daughter's beaded sweatshirt, you'll know where to look for the instructions.)

IRONING EQUIPMENT

Ironing board
Iron and a backup iron (in case the first one goes on the blink)
Spray starch
Water in a spray bottle
Lint brush
Hangers

LAUNDRY SCHEDULE

- When there are just two of you, doing a wash once or twice a week is sufficient. Once you start adding children, everything changes.

- You may find it easier to do a little every day. Start a load in the morning before breakfast and transfer it after the morning dishes are done. To fold only one load of clothes takes just a few minutes.

- Be certain all family members have an adequate supply of socks and underwear to get from washday to washday.

BEFORE YOU WASH

- Most families need to mark their clothing to avoid laundry-room mix-ups. Keep permanent markers on hand (one in your sewing kit and an extra in the kitchen), and note name or initials on the label before the first wearing.

- Laundry hampers should be placed in the rooms where family members regularly take off clothing. The bathroom or bedroom is a logical location. Keep a mesh bag near each hamper so you can sort out hand wash immediately.

- Teach your children (and spouse!) to turn things right side out as they remove clothing so that you don't have to do it. Socks should not go into the wash wadded into balls.

  TIME SAVER

- Store a prewash product on a shelf near the hamper. As your little ones undress, spray-treat stained clothing to save you time when you do the wash. Older kids should be taught to do this for themselves. (Choose a prewash product that doesn't require that the item be washed immediately.)

- For tougher stains—such as those on baby clothes—soak the garment as soon as it's removed.

- Ask older children to take their hampers to the laundry room and sort the clothes among the baskets for dark and white colors and hand laundry. Work out a regular schedule so that your children know that all dirty clothing must be in by 8 A.M. Monday and 8 A.M. Thursday, for example.

  WORTH THE TIME

- Check all pockets and shake out linings to remove lint and other debris. Put found items in the empty canister you've set aside for that purpose.

- Take a stitch in anything that needs mending; it will take only a minute and will extend the life of the clothes.

- Unfold pant cuffs and brush out dirt.

- Close zippers, button up, tie sashes or drawstrings, and fasten Velcro so that none will snag other clothing.
- Turn delicate items inside out for safer washing.
- To get white socks and T-shirts as clean as possible, scrub with a bar of soap first.

SOCK MANAGEMENT

1. Link pairs with a safety pin.
2. Put all socks in a mesh bag to keep them from getting stuck in sheets or towels.
3. If socks do get separated, put the lone sock into its owner's drawer. When you find the missing sock, you'll know where the original one is and can reunite the pair. Or if the missing sock is never found, you may eventually find that you have two lone socks of the same color and can create a new pair.
4. If you have three members of the family who wear similar socks, have them separate socks by owner and put in separate mesh bags. When you take them out, you'll know who owns the socks.
5. Or use a dot of a specific color of nail polish on the bottom of the toe to identify a sock's owner.
6. If there are more socks in your household than you care to manage, establish a bin in the laundry room for clean pairs of socks. Family members can come and identify their own pairs.

FOLDING AND PUTTING AWAY

- To avoid unnecessary ironing, fold items immediately after they come out of the dryer.

- Fold sheets and pillow cases as one unit with the fitted sheet acting as a holder for the other sheet and pillow case. Folding as a set also works well with underwear, pajamas, and baby sets.

- Place folded clothing in the appropriate basket for distribution to the bedrooms. Older children can be instructed to pick up their own baskets and put the clothing away, and then return baskets to the laundry room.

- To rotate wear on clothing—especially articles such as underwear and T-shirts—put freshly washed clothing on the bottom of the pile as you put it away in drawers or on closet shelves. This will help prevent owners from wearing the same pajamas or T-shirts over and over.

- Don't let folded laundry pile up. Put it away as soon as you have a day's laundry completed.

IF YOU USE A LAUNDROMAT OR A COMMUNITY LAUNDRY CENTER

- Trips to a laundromat or apartment-house laundry center are time consuming, so you'll want to do what you can to reduce the number of times you must do the wash:

  —Estimate how often you will need to do the laundry and then set a schedule. If you can get away with only doing the laundry once a week so much the better! Pick your laundry day and time by investigating when the laundry center is the least crowded.

  —Invest in any clothing (socks, underwear, etc.) that will permit all family members to get from washday to washday without needing anything.

  —If, in an emergency, one of you needs a certain item before the next time you wash, consider whether it is easier to launder it by hand rather than trying to fit in an extra wash for the week.

- Establish a jar or dish for laundry money and label it. (Remind family members that this money is for laundry only!) When you come home with spare change, use it to replenish the laundry money. If you still sometimes run out of coins, get a roll of quarters when you do your banking.

- Laundering will be easier if you use a bucket or plastic basin for soaking badly soiled items throughout the week.

- For getting to and from the laundry, purchase a wire mesh shopping cart on wheels. It will be spacious enough to carry family laundry to laundry center and back. Line it with a large plastic bag so that small items won't fall out.

- Before leaving home, presort the laundry. Place the different categories in plastic bags and then place these in the shopping cart.

- Wear a belt bag to conveniently hold the coins you'll need.

- Take with you:

  —Detergent

  —Bleach

  —Fabric softener

  —Several hangers

  —A food-storage size plastic bag (for sock sorting) for each member of the family, labeled by name. The bags can be used week after week.

  —Reading material or something to do if you plan to wait while the laundry is washed

- Wipe out the machine before putting in your clothing.

- To minimize wrinkling, you should fold your laundry as it comes out of the dryer. Use the hangers for clothing that will be hung.

- As you fold, categorize the clothing by family member.

- Pair up socks and put them in the plastic bag with their owner's name on it. When you get back home, you needn't reexamine each pair of socks to determine the owner.

- To load the cart efficiently, start with the towels, then add sheets, and then finally the clothes.

10
LIST MAKING

WHAT'S AHEAD

Your Master List
Creating Your Daily "To Do" List
List Management

When I first met my husband, he had so many lists he had to keep lists of his lists! These little treasures would pop up everywhere: on a closet shelf, in a desk drawer, on the kitchen counter, or in last winter's overcoat. No wonder things never got done.

Here's what I taught him about list making:

TWO RULES OF LIST MAKING:

1. Maintain only one major list for home and personal tasks. (A separate grocery list is the exception.)
2. Use this Master List to create your daily "To Do" list.

YOUR MASTER LIST

- Set up a spiral notebook for keeping track of all the errands and tasks that need to be done—from returning library books and making dental appointments to photocopying canceled checks and going to the shoemaker. By using a notebook, you'll have all your information in one place—no more lists on little scraps of paper.

- Set up sections for your Master List, allowing a page or a half page per section. Logical headlines include: "To Do," "To Buy," "To Call," and "To Ask Spouse About."

- Break major tasks into parts to create a step-by-step action plan. Suppose you're throwing a surprise birthday party for a friend. You will need to: check the date, make a guest list, pick a location, buy and send invitations, plan the menu, arrange for decorations, pick up a gift, order the cake, and so on. All these steps can be written down as separate tasks.

- Also refer to Chapter 14, The Personal Computer; E-mail, Faxes, and Cell Phones; and Home Organization, if you're interested in using your computer for calendar and list management.

CREATING YOUR DAILY "TO DO" LIST

While a Master List includes all the things you would like to get done in the near future, your daily list should include only those items you expect to accomplish in a day.

- Planning should be done the night before. Allow ten minutes to outline your schedule for the next day.

- You will need your Master List and your daily appointments calendar. The calendar should be large enough to accommodate each day's "To Do" list.

  1. Review your current day's "To Do" list. Should any of the undone tasks be carried over to the next day?

  2. Review your calendar. Note activities and meetings for the next few days. Do you need to prepare for any of the upcoming events? If you note that you're bringing lasagna to a potluck dinner on Friday, add the ingredients to the week's shopping list and schedule in time to prepare it later in the week. Or you may have a community meeting for which you need to do some reading or phoning. Add those activities to your "To Do" list now.

3. Review locations of any appointments. Take care of tasks based on where you'll be. If tomorrow's dental appointment is near the tailor, add "Take suit for alterations" to your daily "To Do" list.

4. Review your time. If you see that you have an extra hour in the afternoon, choose a task you can complete in that block of time.

LIST MANAGEMENT

When a list becomes too overwhelming, it's time to take a good look at what you can realistically expect to accomplish. Evaluate each item. If it's a low-level priority, perhaps you can drop it. Or what about hiring someone else to do it for you?

With the tasks that remain, decide what needs to be done right away and schedule them in as soon as possible. The other holdover items should be tackled as soon as your first priorities have been accomplished.

11

THE MAIL

WHAT'S AHEAD

Establishing A System
How to Process:
Magazines • Appointment Reminders/Changes
Catalogs • Correspondence
Bills • Brochures • Solicitations
Cards and Miscellaneous • Invitations
How to Reduce Incoming Mail

*For information on handling e-mail, see
Chapter 14: The Personal Computer; E-mail, Faxes,
and Cell Phones; and Home Organization*

"**M**ail Order Is Booming!" scream the business headlines. What that has meant to us over the last few years is an overwhelming increase in the amount of mail we receive—multiple copies of catalogs, special mailings, and contests—more paper than anyone wants to have to process each day.

If you want to avoid the plight of one of my clients who had to make pathways among the stacks of paper in her apartment, process it you must. Every day. Or you'll simply drown in special offers.

ESTABLISHING A SYSTEM

- When the mail arrives, it should be sorted into piles for the appropriate family members.

- Establish a set place for putting the mail for each person. Use a central hall table, or put it in the appropriate person's room. (If a family member is away, stack the mail according to date received—oldest on bottom—or place his or her mail, organized by date, in a manila envelope.)

- Do not try to manage your own mail until you have five to fifteen minutes to do it properly. There's nothing wrong with *Important!* plucking out and reading that letter from your son as soon as it comes—everyone likes to read the "good stuff" first. Just be sure to take time later in the day to make decisions about the rest of the mail.

- Pick a convenient location to read the mail. At your desk? At the kitchen table? (If you stand up at one of these locations, you'll get the job done faster!) Have at hand a letter opener, a pen, some adhesive-backed notes, and a wastebasket. Take your mail and go through it quickly to toss out what you can. Immediately toss:

  —Solicitations from organizations to which you would never give money

  —Catalogs that don't interest you (If it's a catalog that's new to you, a quick glance at two or three pages will tell you if it's of possible interest. If not, into the wastebasket it goes.)

  —Letters that look like bogus contest announcements (You know: "You've already won a new car! All you need to do is call us at this number within 24 hours. . . .")

- With luck, this first step has winnowed your pile considerably. Now go through the items one by one and evaluate them.

- If you need to check something with another family member, adhesive-backed notes are invaluable. Attach one to the bill or letter in question, and write down your query. (On the phone bill: "Did you call Tallahassee on 12/9 or is this an error?")

- Here are some typical items you might receive and what you should do with them:

Magazines

- If you subscribe to a magazine for pleasure, set it aside to read

FOUR RULES FOR MAGAZINE MANAGEMENT

1. Check your stack of magazines regularly, preferably once a week, but absolutely once a month.

2. Create an "On-the-Go" Reading File. As you go through your magazines, rip out articles that interest you. Each day, select several articles to take with you, and catch up on your reading during moments when you have to wait. (Be selective about what you put in this file. If you rip out too many articles without setting aside specific times to read them, you may simply have created a thinner pile that will also never be read.) Travel and waiting time offer the best opportunities to catch up on your reading, so be sure to have your file with you at those times.

3. Sort and toss what you now realize you'll never read.

4. Think through magazine renewals carefully. Interests—and magazines— change.

when you're relaxing. A shelf in your bedroom or a magazine rack in the living room might be a good spot for placing this leisure-time reading. To prevent pileup: weekly magazines should be read within a week; monthlies should be read within a month. Toss the old one if a new one arrives before you've read it, and consider not renewing when your subscription expires.

- A magazine you read for business should go in your briefcase or near your desk. How to find time to read it? Establish a system. If you commute by bus or train, read one weekly magazine Tuesday mornings; another can be reviewed Thursdays on the commute home. Non-commuters should set aside specific times to go through this reading material regularly.

- If you know of an organization (your local library or senior center?) that collects old magazines, save those you might have thrown out and donate them.

Catalogs

Mail-order shopping is a very efficient way to take care of many of your household, personal, and gift needs. Unfortunately, shopping by mail goes hand in hand with being deluged by catalogs, since customer names are generally sold to other companies. You'll hear regularly from the catalogs you love as well as the ones that hope you'll love them, too. There are several steps to take to keep the household from drowning in slick paper.

- Sort through incoming catalogs daily. Those that don't interest you should go in the trash; those that you'd like to glance through should be looked at or set aside for leafing through while watching television or just before bed.

- Turn down the corners of pages or use adhesive-backed notes to mark pages on which you liked the merchandise. Circle the item number in red ink to find it quickly when you take out the catalog again. File the catalog in a "To Order" file for a week or so until you have a few catalogs from which to order. Then you can do it all at once. As you review what you marked, you may decide against the purchase, or if you'd been watching for a specific item, you may have found it in more than one catalog, and now you can compare prices.

- Keep a record of your order. Photocopy an order sent in the mail or keep a faxed order. If you order by telephone, date the catalog and write your order number and total cost on the outside of the catalog. File the order information in an "Items on Order" file so you can check to be certain that all merchandise was received.

- If you've just ordered sheets for the bedroom, automatically toss all bedding catalogs that arrive in the near future. Also throw out any catalog that comes within a month of the time when you ordered. You'll avoid temptation and save yourself time

TIME SAVER

Bills

- When a bill comes in, circle the date it's due, and put it in your "Bills" file in chronological order. (See Chapter 6, Household Files, for more details.) Set one or two specific dates for paying bills each month, and process all accumulated bills at that time. Paying bills at set times is more efficient than paying them piecemeal, and you'll always have payments in on time because you have a system.

- If you're processing several department-store bills as well as one or two major credit-card bills, consider consolidating the use of your charge cards. Most department stores now accept the major bank cards, and if you use only one or two cards, it reduces mail received, bills to process, and the number of checks you have to write.

Solicitations for Donations

- Any solicitation from an organization to which you'd like to consider giving money should be filed with your bills. Some people like to take care of these donations monthly; others prefer to do it every few months.

- After paying the bills to cover family overhead, you can now take a look at the organizations vying for your dollar. As you decide whether to give to nature preservation or the homeless (or a little to both), toss out those requests you don't expect to be able to fulfill any time soon.

- When you process these solicitations, keep a running list (if your family finances are on a computer, the computer will do it for you) of whom you've given money and the month and year. The organization to which you sent your annual contribution in February will likely start soliciting you again the following fall. If you don't have an easy way to check the date of your last donation, you may end up donating an "annual" gift to them every seven to nine months. Fine, if you intend to; not so fine, if there are other places you'd like to give money. By keeping track, you'll have tight control over your donations.

	200_		
1/17	Whale Adoption	contribution	$45.00
1/17	Save the Children	contribution	$100.00
1/17	League of Women Voters	contribution	$25.00
3/19	Friends of the Library	contribution	$25.00
3/19	Art Museum	contribution	$25.00
4/10	Zoological Society	contribution	$35.00

- If several of your donations involve membership cards (such as museum or zoological-park cards), set up a file for such items. Or if you want to have them handy, put them in your wallet or credit-card case.

Invitations

- If the invitation involves you alone, RSVP immediately, and enter the information in your calendar (and the Family Calendar, if appropriate). Often the original information can be thrown out, but if it has directions or other information you might need, file it in your "Tickler" file (see Chapter 6, Household Files) so that you'll have it when it's needed.

- If a child must be consulted, place it on your desk or a location in the kitchen where you go through scheduling questions with family members.

- If your spouse must be consulted, leave it in the proper mail pile, noting your thoughts on attending.

Dental or medical appointment reminders and changes of address

- If you are processing the mail during the daytime, call immediately to set up appointments. If it's evening, write the numbers on your "To Do" list for the next day.

- Miscellaneous information such as a notice of a change of address or notification of an upcoming meeting should be acted upon as quickly as possible. Note the information in your address book or calendar and throw out the original.

Correspondence

- Read the letter. If it requires a written reply, note your response on the letter while your mind is still focused on the issue at hand. If you're at your desk, you may want to write the reply at once. If not, place the "to be answered" letter in a "To Do" pile for the next day.

- You may prefer to handle personal correspondence at a more leisurely pace. Set the letter aside until you have extra time. If you have a considerable number of letters of this type, establish a "Correspondence" file.

- When you send items of interest (clippings? photographs?) to relatives to whom you write regularly, prepare an envelope for that person as soon as you have something special to send. Use an adhesive-backed note to add an explanation, if necessary, and place the items in the preaddressed envelope. The envelope can now be set aside for a few days until you have time to write the accompanying letter.

- If you have something to send to someone with whom you don't usually correspond, address the envelope, add a quick note, and mail it right away. Otherwise, it will never leave your household.

Brochures of interest

- For certain items—a travel brochure, the winter ballet schedule, or an ad specifying the days the circus will be in town—you may not be able to commit yourself immediately. If you'd really like to go, pencil in the dates in question on your calendar so that you won't book anything else in the meantime. File the brochure in a "Tickler" file so that it will pop out at the time you think you'll be able to decide.

Birthday, holiday, or anniversary cards

- Opening and immediately tossing away someone's wishes for your happiness is a bit hard to do. Some people like to display cards or collect them to show to other family members. This is fine, but set a limit—perhaps seven days after the event—on how long you keep them. If a card has a thoughtful note or special message from an old friend or loved one, save it and store it in your "Mementoes" box or file.

- Some organizations recycle holiday cards by cutting up the cards to make new ones. If you hear of one of these organizations, send them your cards. This offers a thoughtful way to share all your good wishes.

HOW TO REDUCE INCOMING MAIL

If your unsolicited direct-mail intake is more than you want, try writing to: Mail Preference Service, Direct Marketing Association, P.O. Box 9008, Farmingdale, NY 11735-9008, and ask to be removed from their mailing lists. Provide them with the variations of your name that mailing lists are using (Joan G., J.G., Joan . . . etc.). Your name will be put on a Mail Preference Service List that is circulated among national direct-mail companies, which will then remove your name from their lists. If you shop by mail, however, you may find that this reduces your intake only slightly—companies from whom you order will still keep sending you catalogs, and local advertisers don't necessarily get copies of the DMA's Mail Preference list. Here are other steps to take:

- If you receive multiple copies of the same catalog, write or call the company and ask them to send you just one. (It benefits the environment, your postal carrier's back, and your own load of trash.) Give the names to whom the catalogs are coming (e.g., Joan G. Smith, J. G. Smith, and Joan Smith).

- Create a form letter requesting that your name be removed from a company's mailing list. (You can generate a computer form letter, or write or type a letter to be photocopied.) Send it to catalog companies and charities from whom you receive a great deal of unwanted mail. If you include your mailing label, it will help facilitate this process.

- When you order by mail or donate money, note that you don't want your name sold to other companies. (Some catalogs have a box you can check if you don't want to be placed on mailing lists they sell.)

12
MEAL PLANNING

WHAT'S AHEAD

Meal Planning
Supermarket Shopping Made Simple
Coupons
Food Management at Home
Cooking Tips

I have a friend who never plans anything more than a minute in advance. She's so consistent in her non-planning I shouldn't have been surprised at a telephone conversation we had. While we were talking, I mentioned that I was unpacking eight bags of groceries.

"How do you carry home eight bags?" she exclaimed.

"Carry?" I said. "1 buy all my groceries once a week and have them sent home [a common procedure in cities]. What do you do?"

"Oh," said this mother of two, "I can't plan. l shop every night on my way home from work."

If you are now planning your meals day to day, this chapter is for you. It will save you time, you'll avoid last-minute shopping, and you won't run out of ingredients when you're cooking.

MEAL PLANNING

- Once a week, plan all the meals you will serve for the next seven days. Consider who is generally home on what nights, and keep in mind that you shouldn't expect to prepare anything elaborate for the night you have to be at a 7:30 meeting.

- Always plan a couple of backup meals. Plans change, and kids are finicky. A simple meal such as pasta is ideal because you can hold over the ingredients from week to week.

- Plan to double recipes for foods such as meat loaf. Then you can freeze half for another night.

- Plan meals that dovetail with each other to save time and reduce cleanup chores. If you're fixing chicken on Sunday night, bake enough so that you can fix chicken-salad sandwiches for lunch on Monday. Some vegetable dishes can be managed similarly. By cooking a few extra potatoes for supper one night, you'll have half the work done for serving potato salad later in the week.

- Create a chart of your dinner plans:

Sun.	Mon.	Tues	Wed.	Thurs.	Fri.	Sat.
Turkey	Turkey Vegetable Soup	pasta	meat loaf	vegetable lasagna	fish	dine out
potatoes		salad	rice	salad	lentil and bean salad	
	rolls					
vegetables			salad			
	salad				vegetables	
salad						

By writing everything down, you no longer have to remember from day to day what is to be served. After you've used each week's chart, save it in your Household Notebook. Some families like to repeat the same cycle of meals in another four to six weeks.

- If you have unexpected leftovers, take a quick look at your meal chart and write down the best day on which to use them. This method puts leftovers on the table rather than leaving them to grow mold in the back of the refrigerator.

SUPERMARKET SHOPPING MADE SIMPLE

- Whether you shop only for yourself or for a family of six, establish a regular day for doing your major grocery shopping. (If you buy large economy quantities and pick up fresh food at specialty shops as needed, you may be able to go every other week, but the days should still be set in advance.) By setting up a routine, you'll find it easier to keep your kitchen well stocked.

- Choose the day and time based on the following:

  —Best day for coupons or discounts

  —Best day for finding the store well stocked

  —Best time for avoiding crowds

- Shop alone when possible. Children will distract you, and they inevitably beg for items you could live without. (If you have no choice but to bring them, refer to our previous book, *Organize Your Family!*)

- To shop efficiently, draw up a chart of food items according to your store's layout. You'll do far less backtracking for forgotten items, and it will be easier to delegate shopping to another family member or a household employee.

SAMPLE SHOPPING LIST ▶

- Make photocopies. (File the original list in your Household Notebook to save for making future copies.) Choose a convenient place in the kitchen to keep your grocery list and a pen.

- Teach family members to note needed items under the appropriate category headings, writing them down when you are low, not out.

- Write down **every**thing to avoid forgetting things. On a busy day, you may neglect to pick up paper towels if you've forgotten to write it down.

- Make and keep handy a list of ingredients that go into some of your family's favorite dishes. (Store this list in your Household Notebook for easy reference.) A quick glance at this list will tell you what you need to buy for a specific recipe.

AISLE 1	AISLE 2	AISLE 3	AISLE 4	AISLE 5	AISLE 6
Fruits	Canned goods	Seasonings	Dairy	Soups	Frozen foods
Vegetables	Condiments	Household cleaners	Juices	Flour, Sugar	Meats
Baked goods	Crackers, cookies	Paper goods	Breakfast food	Pet food	Fish
Breads	Rice, pasta	Drinks	Snacks		

- Refer to your recipes, and note on your shopping list all ingredients you will need for each dish.

- Leave room in your pantry and freezer so that you can take advantage of sales and coupon specials.

- When you go to the grocery, take along a small calculator so that you can compare per-unit costs or keep a running tab of what you're spending.

- At the cash register, help pack your own groceries so that you can **TIME SAVER** put together items that are stored together—all paper supplies for the upstairs bathroom would go in one bag, frozen items in another, fruits and vegetables together, and so on.

- Look for grocery stores that let you order by phone and deliver, or consider a food service that offers shopping by phone. Then you need only make trips to the store for perishables or those items you want to select for yourself.

FOOD MANAGEMENT AT HOME

- When you arrive home from the grocery, you can prepare for the week by doing more than just putting the food away. Also:

ORGANIZATION +

—Sponge off bottles and cans as you unpack. Dirt collects on the bottoms and will soil your cabinet or refrigerator if you don't wipe them clean.

—If meat will be used in smaller portions, divide it up now, label, date, and freeze.

—If your refrigerated juice supply is low, mix up a new can of frozen juice, using a fresh container.

—Wash the lettuce, spin it dry, and store in a cloth salad bag or crisper.

—Clean, cut, and refrigerate vegetables such as celery and carrots. Storing carrot and celery sticks in water will keep them fresh

—If you don't use a great deal of cheese, slice and freeze it in appropriate-sized portions.

—Prepare snack-size portions of food such as chips or pretzels for packed lunches.

—Make the tuna salad for tomorrow's lunch.

—Mix up meat loaf for tonight now. Refrigerate and bake later.

• Plan for the time to get these tasks done after you shop. When you're in a squeeze, finish while preparing dinner.

COUPONS

- Purchase a coupon organizer through a catalog or at a local five-and-dime store. By having a convenient way to store and retrieve coupons, you'll use them more effectively.

- Coupons should be clipped and filed on the day the advertisement arrives in your home.

- File by category. If you have an extensive number of coupons for one type of product, arrange them in chronological order by expiration date. Mark the coupon expiration date with a highlighter, or circle with a red pen, so that you can see at a glance what the final date is.

- After evaluating your shopping list, preselect coupons to take with you.

- Remember that coupons save you money only if the product is used. If your family hates the toothpaste that has coupons, you're better off paying the extra few cents for the brand they prefer.

- If you have extra coupons you won't be able to use, donate them. Libraries and senior centers sometimes have boxes set out for coupon exchange; you can also leave them at the store on the shelf next to the item.

COOKING TIPS

- Delegate tasks to family members. Have them set the table, wash vegetables, or prepare a salad in advance. If you won't be home when they come in, leave a note.

- Establish a baking or a cooking day. Once you're in the kitchen, it's easy to dovetail projects: the shortening for the cookies can be softening while you finish making the casserole.

- Before cooking from a recipe, always read it all the way through so that there won't be surprises as you go along.

- Use a kitchen timer when baking. It's easy to get distracted and burn your hard work.

- You've just realized that the margarine stick you unwrapped is your last, but your hands are too sticky to add it to the list now. What to do? Leave the empty box or wrapper on the counter. When you're wiping up (and your hands are clean), you'll spy the wrapper and be reminded to add "margarine" to your list.

- Clean up and put away as you go along. When you're ready to start the new dish, you'll find things where they're supposed to be and counter surfaces will be usable.

- When cleaning up after baking or cooking or after the evening meal, work systematically. Start with the least cluttered counter and work around the room until the items on each counter have been processed and the counter wiped clean.

- Double duty:

—Get two items off your list at the same time. Make a phone call while you're grating carrots or rinsing dishes. Use a speaker phone or cradle the receiver between ear and shoulder when you need both hands free.

—Waiting for something to finish baking? Wipe down the refrigerator shelves, empty the dishwasher, write a note, or check your meal chart to see if there's a chore you can take care of for one of the meals in the next few days.

—Share cooking responsibilities with a friend. You love to bake and hate to cook, and she loves to cook and hates to bake? Divide up chores and share equally.

13
MEAL PLANNING: RECIPES

WHAT'S AHEAD

Recipe Management
Other Recipe Tips

Have you ever noticed that great cooks often don't use recipes? The aromas that wafted from my neighbor's home when I was growing up sometimes made me want to go there for what I imagined would be a delectable afternoon snack. Yet her recipe box was in shambles. Recipes were uncategorized and stuffed in so tightly I couldn't imagine how she ever took one out.

For those of us mortals who like to refer to recipes now and then, there needs to be a system that gets them out of the magazines and ovenside so that we can try them.

RECIPE MANAGEMENT

This system allows you to store untried recipes while adding those that you like to a personalized cookbook:

- Purchase:

    —Looseleaf binder

    —Paper for binder

    —Tabbed divider pages **with pockets**

    —Photo album pages with plastic overlays (for use with a looseleaf binder) to hold the recipes. As you build your personalized cookbook, you'll have recipes on spill-proof pages.

- Label divider pages by category: "Appetizers," "Chicken," "Pasta," "Desserts," etc. If you have a special interest, such as low-cholesterol dishes or barbecuing, create categories for those recipes.

- Assemble your new cookbook as follows: After each divider page, put several photo-album pages. The album pages will display the recipes you've tried and liked. Untried but interesting recipes you've saved (Chocolate Mousse) should be placed in the pocket of the divider page with the appropriate heading ("Desserts").

- If you have many recipes, create a separate binder for each category: "Appetizers," "Pasta Dishes," "Desserts," etc.

- Any new recipe you keep should be photocopied so that it's all on one page (not on pieces torn from a magazine). Photocopying will also keep the recipe from smudging.

- On a copy of any recipe:

    —Highlight any ingredients you don't normally have on hand.

    —Note preparation time, pot or pan used, and any special suggestions for the next time.

    —Also write down comments: Did the kids love it? Is it a company dish? Did it go particularly well with a certain side dish?

By making a few notes about a recipe, you will save time and improve future results.

- Favorite family recipes should be stored in the binder as well. If you've used an index-card system in the past, photocopy front and back of the card, and insert the entire recipe under an overlay. That way you won't have to remove the card to read instructions on the back.

- Is this the fifth recipe for cheesecake you've cut out and not tried? Sort through your collection, and keep only the one or two that sound best and easiest. Note on your shopping list the ingredients you'll need, so that you can try it soon.

- Remove old recipes from the binder when you've tried new and better ones for the same dish.

- When looking for recipes in cookbooks, do you ever forget which book contains a specific recipe? Here's a solution. In the front of your binder, dedicate one page to keeping track. Note the name of the dish, the cookbook it's in, and the page number. That way you can locate all your favorite recipes.

OTHER RECIPE TIPS

- Most kitchens don't have space for an extensive cookbook collection. If there is no room to add shelving in the kitchen or a nearby utility room, then keep only your personal binder and a few of your most frequently used cookbooks in the kitchen. Store the remainder of your cookbooks elsewhere in the house.

- If you prefer an index-card file-box method (broken into categories, of course), here are some time-saving suggestions.

—Don't recopy recipes from magazines by hand. Clip the recipe, photocopy it to reduce smearing, and paste it to an index card.

—Put a select number of favorite recipes on colored cards. When you reach into the "Bread" section, you can quickly put your fingers on the card with your favorite banana bread recipe because you know it's one of the two or three recipes under "Bread" that is on a pink card.

14

THE PERSONAL COMPUTER; E-MAIL, FAXES, AND CELL PHONES; AND HOME ORGANIZATION

WHAT'S AHEAD

Computer Basics

Organizational Strengths of the Computer

Backing Up Isn't Hard

The World at Your Fingertips

The Convenience of E-mail

Home Faxes

The Cell Phone Generation

"I want to use my home computer to help me get better organized" is a comment I'm hearing more and more often. People seem to think that these electronic wonders are going to do everything from straightening out their home finances to brewing their coffee in the morning! Personal computers do not yet operate as home robots, but they can help you be better organized.

COMPUTER BASICS

- If you're buying a new computer, purchase the most recent model. Technology is changing so rapidly you should start out with the most up-to-date model so that it will be compatible with software programs to come.

- Be sure your computer has a warranty. If a problem is going to occur, it generally happens within the first few months.

- To operate your computer, you can select programs that run by using key-stroke commands—similar to using a typewriter. Or you can select software that is graphics-based and runs primarily by use of a "mouse." Buy the form that makes you the most comfortable. People who have used typewriters for years are sometimes uncomfortable with the eye-hand coordination needed for the mouse. Other people swear by the mouse-based programs.

- If you're selecting new software, ask for a demonstration to be certain the program has the features you want. Also ask if the program's company offers a toll-free customer support number.

- To learn about computers:

  1. Take a course. To get the most out of it, you'll need access to a computer on which to practice.

  2. Go to the bookstore or a computer store and browse through the computer books looking for ones that pertain to the programs you're using. Some of them are directed at helping even the most computer phobic, so watch for those that look easy and useful. (Ask store personnel for recommendations.)

  3. Subscribe to one of the computer magazines. Purchase several at a newsstand and select the one that best meets your needs.

  4. Ask friends or inquire at the store where you bought the computer for the name of a student or a computer consultant who would come to your home. You've made a substantial investment in buying the computer. If you hire someone to get you started, it can be money well spent—your consultant can explain exactly what you want and need to know.

- Anytime you invest in a new software program or add a feature to your computer, set aside time to become familiar with it. Many programs come with tutorials that are worth working through, and as with any other product, you'd be amazed at what reading the operating instructions will do for you. If you're still stumped, an hour with a tutor can get you up and running.

- Be realistic about how you anticipate using your computer. They are wonderful for all types of word-processing chores and terrific for money management, but if you're a person who finds that technology hinders, not helps you, then recognize that you may not yet aspire to do everything by computer. Later, as you become more comfortable with the technology, you may want to use it more fully.

- If children will be using your computer, invest in one of the programs that prohibits them from entering your files. There are several that give children free access to all material intended for them but let only the adult password holders go beyond to information such as family finances.

- Invest in a good backup system that is easy to use. The single biggest mistake people make in using their computers is failing to back it up. You may not have a problem for years, but a breakdown can happen, and losing years' worth of data is devastating.

ORGANIZATIONAL STRENGTHS OF THE COMPUTER

Address Book: The computer is an ideal place to store names and addresses because the information is easy to update and easy to categorize. For example, if you're visiting Colorado and want a print-out of all your friends in the Denver area, your computer can sort and create this list for you. However, most of us would find it inconvenient to have to turn on the computer every time we needed an address, so the solution to the need-it-in-a-second dilemma is to print out a complete copy of your address book periodically and store the print-out in a looseleaf binder near your desk. That way it's easy to look up an address or two, and the book itself can be updated in a jiffy—just print out a new page whenever you make changes. (Entering all your addresses into the computer is a painstaking process. Establish some mini-goals such as putting in ten addresses a day or consider hiring someone to do it for you.)

"Boilerplate" letters and **word-processing chores:** If you enjoy writing to companies for information or sending out a holiday letter about your family, you can save time on letter writing by using a form letter and adding personalized information when you need to. And, of course, any typing chores are greatly simplified because it's so easy to edit.

Calendar planner programs: Some people are beginning to use these instead of date books. Most of these programs have some excellent features: "to do" list management, which makes it possible for tasks to be carried over until completed; a permanent birthday and anniversary chart integrated into your calendar; and the ability to reschedule appointments without reentering all the data. (You simply move an appointment, complete with person's name and number and any notes you may have made about the meeting.) A drawback to a calendar/planner on a computer is that most of us aren't with our computers all the time. Though you can print out pages to take with you, it's not like having your whole date book at hand. Portable computers weighing two to eight pounds are now available and help solve that problem, but that's an added expense. One client who had a home computer decided that the best way to enter the electronic age was to test a calendar/planner program on the home computer she already had. If she's in love with it, then she'll make the investment in a smaller, handier computer she can take with her.

If you try to convert from a paper calendar to one on computer, remember everything takes time. You may like the way you can manage your long-range "to do" list with the computer, but dislike the telephone-directory aspect of it. The most organized approach is to use the aspects that work for you.

Family finances: Get financial software recommendations from friends whose situations are similar to yours. The best program will be one that addresses the specifics you need to track: Do you follow stock investments? Do you run a home-based business? Do you have in-home employees on whom records must be kept? In general, a financial program will help in several ways. It will:

—Function as your electronic checkbook, noting both income and expenses, and neatly categorize them for tax time and other purposes. You needn't turn on your computer every time you write a check, but do set up a routine for entering data every few days. (Use a file folder to hold papers with your notations until you've entered the information into the computer.)

—Give you an accurate look at where your money is being spent—ideal for keeping track of your budget.

—Permit you to print out by category, such as organizations to which you've donated money, to assess when and how much you gave them the last time.

—Keep track of payments. If a company says you haven't paid them, you can scan through several months of your paper-based checkbook, looking for the item check by check, or you can go into your computer and let it look for the payment—and it can do it in seconds, not minutes or hours!

Graphics: You can create your own letterhead, or design personalized cards and invitations—all right there on your computer.

Health-insurance forms: To help simplify the increasingly complicated process of filing for reimbursements on medical costs, programs have been developed to help you fill out the required forms and keep records on your claims.

Home decorating: Floor-plan programs let you be the decorator. The program gives you rooms and furniture scaled to your measurements, and you can test different room arrangements without hurting your back. If you have a color monitor, certain programs let you test out different color and pattern combinations within a room.

Household instructions: Enter basic information into a computer once, and modify it as needed. For example, if you have children, create an instruction sheet for nighttime sitters, giving bedtimes, bedtime rituals, emergency numbers, etc. Before printing out, you need only add the number of where you'll be for that particular evening. Or if a child is sick one evening, simply add the medicine dosage and time to the instruction sheet. Other household information that might be worth putting on the computer includes: feeding instructions for the kennel where your dog boards; watering directions for the plant sitter; your personal property inventory; your list of important information, including bank accounts, attorneys, accountants.

Legal needs: There are programs on will-writing as well as programs that give you legal boilerplate letters for leases, powers of attorney, employment agreements, defective product complaint letters, and more.

Mailing lists: If you have a volunteer job that involves doing mailings, the proper printer and software program will be invaluable to you. Some people use mailing labels for holiday cards now, and while they are not my first choice for sending personal mail, you may want to use them if they are the only way you'll get the job done.

Résumés: Programs do the professional setup for you.

Travel: With the right software, your computer can now plot for you the best driving route from Point A to Point B. A printout lets you take the information along on the trip.

BACKING UP ISN'T HARD TO DO

- Purchase an easy-to-use backup system so that it's hassle-free. Failing to back up their computers is the single biggest mistake people make, so back up your data regularly (monthly is generally adequate for home computers). If you've come to rely on your computer, loss of data is devastating. Write a reminder note to yourself at the first of each month, and be sure the backup gets done.

- If something important goes on your computer mid-month, copy that information onto a separate disk or run a complete mid-month backup.

THE WORLD AT YOUR FINGERTIPS

It will take you only a few visits to the Internet to realize the vast possibilities it offers. (In all likelihood, you've had some experience with it at work, even if you're not plugged in at home.) Whether you want to access an airline to check on flight availability, do some research on the colleges your teenager is considering, or move some money from one of your bank accounts to another, the Internet can help you do it in a fraction of the time any one of these tasks would have taken previously. More and more people are beginning to find this is a time-saving tool they don't want to be without.

- Speed of modem is critical in accessing online services and the Internet. If you're working with an older computer, spend the money to upgrade your modem to the fastest one currently available.

- Consider adding an additional phone line for your modem. If you've got a fax, you could combine the two. You'll likely find that it's unrealistic to expect one phone line to provide telephone, fax, and modem service.

- Investigate online services. If no one in the family is likely to use "chat" rooms and some of the other online services, you may prefer to sign up with a commercial "access provider" that, for a fee, will give you a direct link to the Internet.

- If you have children, investigate the parental control features available through online services.

- Visit regularly. The Internet is changing—and improving—constantly. Keep checking out what it has to offer. The more experienced you are at navigating, the faster you'll be able to access what you need.

THE CONVENIENCE OF E-MAIL

E-mail is an easy, fast way to correspond. Once you begin using it, you'll find that a 20-second e-mail can quickly replace a 10-minute phone call. What's more, you don't need stamps, paper, or pen, and a mere click of the mouse will send your message on its way instantly. But because e-mail is somewhat addictive (it's a lot like chatting with friends), you need to control it to be sure it doesn't control you:

- Just as you should set aside specific time to answer your regular mail, do the same with e-mail.

- Scan the incoming messages by order of importance, using the subject line or the sender to make a judgement. If you're running low on time and have not answered all your messages, skim through the remaining list, and do one of three things: 1) answer the more important immediately; 2) save the significant for the next day; 3) delete everything else so you don't waste time on it the next time you log on.

- Keep your own messages clear and to the point. Be specific about what you need to know so that the message you get in return will also be concise.

- E-mail addresses should be kept in your online address book so that you can click and send easily, but also note e-mail addresses in your personal address book so that you can stay in touch even when you're not on your own PC.

Junk mail exists in e-mail form, too. Here's how to stay off the lists:

- Be cautious about giving out your name and e-mail address if you want to limit who you hear from.
- Check out special mail preference services through online services and the Internet to specify that you don't want to be on general mailing lists.
- If you receive unwanted e-mail, notify the sender. They are supposed to remove you from their lists.

HOME FAXES

Another wonderful invention of the past few years has been the fax machine. Like e- mail, messages travel quickly across telephone wires but instead of going into your computer, they materialize on paper—exact replicas of the paper that was sent on the other end of the wire.

In all likelihood, your office fax machine has been around for years, so you're well-accustomed to having one around. If you're considering adding one at home, then here are a few points to keep in mind when you shop:

- The most important feature of your fax machine concerns what kind of paper it uses. The less expensive machines use thermal paper which comes on rolls and tends to curl. This may be the perfect choice for a family who is reading and tossing inter-family faxed communications. If you plan to use a fax machine for business purposes, you're better off selecting a more expensive model that uses plain paper. This will provide you with a better quality of fax to save and refer to over time.

- Ask about other features. All can be used for low-volume copying; some have speed-dialing; most have memory so that an incoming fax can be stored if you are low on toner or out of paper, and many have a "broadcast" feature that permits you to send one fax to several different numbers. New machines being created for the home market are also designed to serve as an answering machine, so keep shopping and listening. They are getting better all the time.

Here are some additional tips for better fax management:

- Fax during off-hours. It's cheaper.

- If you're faxing to another household out-of-state, consider whether or not there is a time change. The relative with the fax machine in her bedroom/office won't be thrilled to get your fax at midnight.

- Just because a fax arrives instantly, it doesn't need to be answered instantly. Just as you manage your mail and e-mail, you have to take charge of when you're going to deal with any faxed messages.

- If junk faxes start arriving in your machine, fax back to the sender to remove you from the list. (The sender's number should appear on the fax that comes through to you.)

THE CELL PHONE GENERATION

A ringing cell phone in the middle of a meeting or during a movie in a public theater is downright annoying, but no one can argue with the convenience of being able to call your dentist's office from your car to say you're stuck in traffic and will be a little late. Being able to call for help in an emergency is also tremendously reassuring. For most people cell phones are a convenience and a comfort—growing more and more to be a necessity. Here are some pointers:

- Shop for size. The new cell phones are so tiny they'll fit in a man's suit pocket creating nary a bulge.

- Make sure you purchase a digital (as opposed to analog) model, they are the way of the future.

- Advanced voice mail, caller ID, call-waiting, call-forwarding, paging and even e-mail are all available with some wireless phones. The extra services mean extra money so buy only what you need.

- If you'll be using your cell phone when traveling, ask about "roaming" charges. These can really add up.

- Give the number out sparingly. You pay for incoming as well as outgoing calls.

- If you anticipate primarily using your phone in the car, then have a car phone installed instead. They offer more power and longer battery life. If you decide on in-car installation, price out auto-dialing and speaker phones. This will increase safety.

- Don't use your cell phone while actively driving. (Sitting in a traffic jam is another thing.) A recent study showed that people are four times more likely to have an accident while talking on a cell phone.

- And if you are attending the theater or going to a meeting, turn off the phone. Out of consideration for others, your calls will just have to wait.

BEEP BEEP

There was a time when only doctors wore beepers. Now everyone--even kids--seem to have them. If you simply need a way for people to get in touch with you, you may find that a beeper (which can be set on "vibrate" during meetings and movies) is more practical for you than a cell phone.

15

PHOTOGRAPHS AND VIDEOTAPES: ORGANIZING MEMORIES

WHAT'S AHEAD

Catching the Perfect Moment

Documenting Your Photographs

Safe Preservation

Taking Home Videos

What to Do When Your Photos
Are in Boxes . . . and Boxes

amily memories are important to all of us. By looking through photographs or watching our own videotapes, we gain a sense of ourselves and a feeling for our family history. It's particularly important to organize these documents of our past so that they can be enjoyed for years to come.

CATCHING THE PERFECT MOMENT

- Choose a convenient location for storing both camera and video camera. Put them away after each use so that you don't miss those perfect moments.

- Keep the camera loaded at all times; have on hand extra film and batteries. Video camera batteries should be put away charged so that the camera is ready when you are.

- Consider adding an instant camera to your collection. Most families find that the fun of seeing the picture right away—and the advantage of not having to shoot a whole roll to develop a few pictures—outweigh the extra cost.

DOCUMENTING YOUR PHOTOGRAPHS

- As soon as you get the photographs back from being developed, note the date on the outside of the envelope and give a short summary of what the set of pictures includes. After the pictures have been placed in albums, your envelope notation—"Grandpa's birthday, Jan. 10, 20— ," for example—can identify the negatives in case you ever want reprints.

- Label each picture as to date, place, and people involved. By doing so, you're creating a more useful document for others.

SMART TIP

- To write on the backs of photos, buy a special marker at a camera store. Pencils or ballpoint pens leave an impression on the front of the photograph; felt-tip pens smear even after the ink is supposed to have dried. (Even with the special marker, don't stack the photos as you write; allow an extra few minutes' drying time.)

- Sort the pictures and put them into an album or scrapbook right away. If you keep up with it, you'll find that it takes only fifteen to twenty minutes per month. If you stuff them into a drawer to do "later," it will take you hours to straighten out. (For advice on getting your pictures out of the drawers and into the albums, keep reading—it's not too late.)

TIME SAVERS

- How to organize the albums? Create one family album, and make copies of favorite pictures for smaller albums, one for each child.

- Consider using a scrapbook instead of a photo album. The blank pages allow you to write notes, impressions about a vacation, or something about what's happening in the photograph. Ticket stubs, locks of hair (next to the photo of the first haircut), and special mementoes can easily be added, making the reading more fun.

- Do you need photographs to send to relatives who live far away? Take advantage of photo company offers to reproduce doubles when the film is developed. Or take several shots of the same event so that you needn't wait for extra prints to send Grandma.

- Create a gallery of framed favorites so that the family can regularly be reminded of certain people, times, and experiences.

- Check your photography store to find fun ways to use your pictures. Some companies will put the photo of your choice on a T-shirt or a mug, or they can build an entire calendar from a dozen of your family photographs. One company is marketing a system for which they will put select shots on a specially designed photo CD that plays through your television set; other companies will put together videotapes of your family photographs, or check around for shops that will post your pictures on the Internet with special access for your family and extended family.

SAFE PRESERVATION

Unfortunately, families are discovering that photographs stored in inexpensive albums with acetate or poly-vinyl chloride covering deteriorate, partly because of the coverings. To ensure preservation:

- Shop for albums and scrapbooks at camera stores or order through specialty mail-order companies. Make certain that the style you choose is marked "archival," or "non-PVC," or "nonacidic."

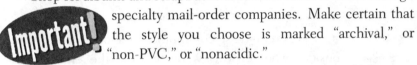

- Don't use cellophane tape or rubber cement when mounting. Both can be damaging.

- Don't store photos in garage, basement, or attic. The fluctuating temperatures cause deterioration, and dampness can cause mold. Store albums, negatives, and extra photographs in a dark closet in the regular part of the house, where temperature and humidity are relatively constant.

- For long-term storage, put photos and negatives in metal cabinets or acid-free boxes. (Wood contains chemicals that can cause photos to deteriorate.)

- What about a very precious picture? Have a studio copy it. Use the copy for display, and store the original, standing vertically, in an acid-free envelope in a climate-controlled portion of the house.

- Take at least one roll of black-and-white film per year. The photographs are less likely to fade over time.

Taking Home Videos

- If you're not yet at ease operating your home video camera, carry a written checklist as to switches, reminders, and settings.

- Prior to a major event (first communion, recital, bar mitzvah), consider whether you want to view the entire event through a lens. If not, ask someone else (cousin? neighborhood teen?) to shoot it for you. Teach him or her how to operate the camera, and before the event, point out important people to catch on tape. Don't leave home without testing the camera first.

WORTH THE TIME

- Most people record too much. Think through what you're going to tape, and see if you can't create a story with a beginning, middle, and end. Birthday, holiday, and vacation narratives will make the viewing more fun.

- Some of the new handycams make it easy to edit a tape as you transfer the film onto videotape. Try to do this within a few days of the taping so that you'll remember the parts you want to edit.

- As special gifts to your children, do ten-minute interviews on their birthdays. When each child turns twenty-one, you'll have a wonderful personal document to present.

- Send video letters to grandparents. You can even tape impromptu performances, the children's artwork, or a block castle they built. And if these "letters" are saved, you'll eventually have a wonderful video album.

- Label all videotapes so that nothing gets recorded over.

- Again, label all videotapes. My brother-in-law doesn't always remember to do this. He says he does, but all I know is that we'll be watching a video of all the cousins playing in the grass, when suddenly in will pop Big Bird on *Sesame Street*. If a tape is labeled when you first use it, no one will grab it to tape your child's favorite program.

- For preservation, store videotapes upright. If you lay them flat, the tape tension relaxes, making for poor quality

WHAT TO DO WHEN YOUR PHOTOS ARE IN BOXES ... AND BOXES

- Set aside several hours each week when you can work **uninterrupted**. (You do not want husbands, wives, sisters, or cousins—and least of all, children, looking over your shoulder and grabbing favorites while you work.)

- Choose a location where you can spread out.

- Go through the house, locating all the places where you've stuffed those photo envelopes, and gather everything together.

- Go through what you've gathered, envelope by envelope (or photo by photo), grouping them by year. If you dated them when you got them, this will be easy. If not, you'll have to work slowly through the stacks. (Set aside any you can't quite date. You can consult other family members later, or perhaps another set of photos will jog your memory as to the likely date.)

- There is no law against throwing out bad pictures: Toss the one of Johnny crossing his eyes and the one of Uncle Harry blinking.

- Once you've gone through each box and grouped the pictures by year, go through each of these groups and place the envelopes chronologically. On each envelope write the year and number the envelopes sequentially. That way if anything gets moved it's easy to refile.

- You now have a logical beginning for placing photos into albums. Work methodically until finished, and label photos as you work.

- Are you trying to sort out years and years worth of photos? To avoid getting discouraged, choose a relatively recent pivotal moment in the family—a birth or a graduation—and start an album with pictures of this event, working forward chronologically until the present time. By getting two or three years' worth organized, you'll find that it will be easier to delve back in "history" to sort out the rest of the family photographs.

- Negatives should be labeled and saved. Purchase boxes for this purpose from your camera store or a specialty catalog. The boxes are designed to preserve the negatives. If the negatives are stored neatly in chronological order (with notes as to the subject matter—"Cape Cod vacation, July 1993," for example), it's easy to pull the negatives to have copies made.

- Send extra photographs and perhaps one set of negatives annually to your parents' or in-laws' home for safekeeping. In the event of a fire or a flood in your home, you have safeguarded a record of your family history by seeing that some pictures will be preserved.

16

TIPS, TIME-SAVERS, AND SHORTCUTS

WHAT'S AHEAD

Household Safety and Emergency Precautions

Household Management

Telephone Tips and Time Savers

Additional Time-savers and Conveniences

Financial Time-savers

The Web: Specializing in Time Savings

Shopping Tips

Clutter Control

The Well-Organized Car

---

ometimes having a better organized home is as simple as learning some new time-savers and shortcuts. Here are some tips for better home management in a variety of areas.

HOUSEHOLD SAFETY AND EMERGENCY PRECAUTIONS

- Make a list (to be stored in your Household Notebook) of the location of the electric meter, water meter, septic tank (or cesspool), propane tank, and any underground utilities. For those items with control panels, note current settings so you'll know what "normal" looks like. You'll be better prepared to handle—or to advise others as they handle—a household emergency.

- Learn about your fuse box or circuit-breaker system. Ask someone to help you identify what fuses or circuit breakers control which parts of the house, and label them. In the event of a problem, you'll know what to do.

- Record the combinations of any locks and also the imprint number of car keys. The imprint number of the key will let the car dealer provide you with a new key if you've lost your set and the spare.

- If you have many keys—or several keys that look alike—have a hardware store or locksmith stamp your keys with numbers: key no. 1 opens the top lock; key no. 2 opens the bottom lock; key no.

3 opens the backdoor, and so on. (For a safe—and organized—approach to your home, have the proper key in hand, ready to unlock the door.)

- Spare keys:

    —Keep a spare car key in your wallet.

    —Give a spare key to nearby relatives. If you are away, they can make an impromptu check on the house.

    —Leave a spare set of house keys with a neighbor who is usually home. Agree with the neighbor on an appropriate "mislabel" of the spare set, such as using your cat's or dog's name. (Don't identify the keys by your address or last name. If the neighbor's home is robbed, the burglars may find your keys and be able to hit two homes in the same night.)

HOUSEHOLD MANAGEMENT

- Every household should designate spots for the following:

    1. A "to do" area (a shelf or closet) that is checked daily. This is where you put the library books that need to be returned at the end of the week (the date should also be marked on your calendar), the candlestick that needs to be glued, the birthday gift that needs to be wrapped.

    2. A permanent place to keep items to donate. If you have a specific shelf, closet, or area of the basement in which to put things, you'll find it easier to get those items out of your house. (As you pack them up, keep a running list of the contents so that you'll have an accurate record for tax purposes.)

3. A specific place for anything you use regularly (glasses, house or car keys, library card, etc.). Then always be certain to put these items back where they belong.

- Set aside a block of time weekly to tend to home-related tasks, wrap gifts, do mending, take appliances to be repaired, put photos in album, all the miscellaneous chores that build up over a week.

- Keep a basket at the foot of the stairs for items that belong upstairs. When you go up, take the basket and spend a few minutes distributing the items. (Don't forget to bring the basket back down with you.)

- Household rules that will make life easier:

  —Make your bed as soon as you get up in the morning.

  —If you take something out, hang it up, file it, or put it away.

  —Take care of things as they occur (wipe out the bathroom sink, straighten up the dining room right after a meal, put away dry cleaning as soon as you come home, send a card as soon as you hear someone is sick).

  —Never go to bed with dirty dishes in the sink.

  —To minimize the amount of dirt that comes through the doors, use good mats outside and rugs inside.

SIMPLIFY CHORES

- Use comforters to reduce time spent making the beds.

- Keep a sponge, spray cleaner, and gloves right in the bathroom to make frequent cleanups easy.

- Store extra trash bags in the bottom of the trash bin so that as soon as you finish with one you can pull out another.

- When you load the dishwasher, put like utensils together so that knives, forks, and spoons will all be grouped for easier unloading.

- Add a twelve-foot extension cord to your vacuum cleaner to reduce the number of times you have to switch outlets.

TELEPHONE TIPS AND TIME-SAVERS

- Manage your telephone time. Set limits on incoming calls and establish a time that's convenient for you to make outgoing calls. By grouping your calling time primarily to one block of the day, it leaves you more time for other things.

- Consider a cordless telephone. These phones are different from cellular phones because their range is limited to about 100 feet from the "home base," but it is great to be able to make a call from anywhere you want—the front porch on a beautiful day or from around the house when you'd like to do some picking up while finishing a conversation.

- If you're intent on organizing your time and your life, then you've got to be willing to take control of the telephone by investing in a home answering machine or voice-mail system. If your dinner hour has been interrupted one too many times by the ringing telephone, you'll likely agree with me that it's as important to control incoming calls when you are there as when you're not!

- If you have several family members living at home, investigate the voice-mail systems that let callers leave messages for specific individuals. That way you don't have to reel through your children's calls trying to track down the business call you were expecting.

- Telephones today have many time-saving features. Look into speed dialing (a system that stores your most frequently called numbers), speaker phone (it leaves your hands free to do other things), automatic redial (this saves you time in redialing), and conference calling (for working out details with several individuals). Also consider whether you're interested in call-waiting, call-forwarding, or caller ID.

A DDITIONAL TIME SAVERS AND CONVENIENCES

- In your sewing basket, keep two needles prethreaded (white and black) at all times. That way, unexpected mending chores can be taken care of in only a few minutes.

- Buy all birthday and anniversary cards for the year in January; preaddress the envelopes and date-file them in your monthly "Tickler" files. (A card for someone with an April 1 birthday should be filed in March so that it's mailed in time.) Buy a few all-occasion cards to have on hand in case you need to send a special "hello," "thank you," or "get well" greeting.

- Save steps around the house by investing in certain convenience items for each room. Scissors, for example, are needed in the kitchen, with the gift-wrapping items, in the sewing basket, and at each spot where you keep desk supplies.

- Spares can also help you be prepared for the unexpected: Keep an umbrella at home, at work, and in the car. Extra pairs of panty hose for women or socks, shirt, and tie for men can come in handy at the office.

- Use a red pen or a highlighter to:

  — Highlight the program listings in your weekly television guide. (You may prefer to record programs to watch at a more convenient time.)

—Make it easier to find telephone numbers in your local telephone directory. Next time you'll be able to find the number quickly.

—Leave an important "Do Not Forget!" note to family members or household help.

—Remind you of things you might forget on your calendar: an important errand, your friend's birthday, etc.

- Carry a small notebook with you to write things down.

- Keep pen and paper in your bedside table for noting down thoughts.

- To simplify bill paying and letter writing, order a rubber stamp with your return address or run off "return address" labels on your computer.

- At your local post office ask how to buy stamps by mail to avoid waiting in line.

- Give yourself a break by hiring help where you can:

—Teens to do leaf raking, cleaning, or errands

—Specialists such as exercise trainers and hair stylists who will come to your home

—Restaurants that will prepare gourmet dinners-to-go

—Caterer for a party

—Personal shopper for your own clothes or for gifts

—Financial planner who will perform a variety of services, from reconciling a checkbook to advising on investments

FINANCIAL TIME SAVERS

- Create a card to carry with you that lists:

    —Bank account numbers

    —Insurance-policy numbers

    —Family social security numbers

- Arrange for your paycheck to be deposited directly into your bank account, and for money to be disbursed to savings automatically.

- Set up electronic disbursement for recurring payments, such as mortgages or insurance premiums, that are unvarying in amount and due date.

- Save check writing time by using:

    —Banks where you can pay bills by phone by punching in the amount and the code as to whom the payment is to be made.

    —Software that offers bill-paying service if you have a modem.

- Do in-person banking at quiet hours. Don't drop in to see your bank officer. Make an appointment first.

THE WEB: SPECIALIZING IN TIME SAVINGS

If you've got an online hook-up for your computer, then you're already saving time and shoe leather because of all the information you can pull into your own home off the Internet. If you're not yet using this powerful tool, then run—don't walk—to anyone who can help you get online. (Upgrade your computer if necessary or hire someone to help get you launched online.) Remember the hours you used to spend at a car dealer's talking about the car you might buy? Today you can do your research and your price-shopping via the Web. Ultimately you can even buy your car online. And as for consumer information, it's a fingertap away: Want to know how to clean a product you've just purchased? Go to the company's web site and leave a message. Most companies get back to you within only a day or two. And if your local library closes at five o'clock and your child informs you he needs to do some research, sit down and go on the Web with him. Chances are excellent you'll find more information than he can possibly use.

One day we'll all view the Internet (the Web) as indispensable as the telephone.

SHOPPING TIPS

- When you buy new clothing and still need to find accessories, snip a tiny piece of fabric from an inside seam and tape it to a card you can carry with you. You'll be able to get a match without taking the entire outfit along.

- To simplify errands, always make a list in advance and lay out what you'll need to take with you. Also:

    —Establish a specific day for doing errands and then consolidate so that you can get everything done at once.

    —Do errands at times when the establishments will be least crowded.

    —Organize errands by location. If the pharmacy is on your route home from work, stop to pick up your prescription.

- Buy items in bulk (shampoo, spray cleaner, detergent, dry dog food, etc.). This saves money, reduces trips to the store, and cuts down on waste. For easier storage, transfer bulk items into smaller containers. A normal shampoo bottle can be saved and rinsed out to use again, for example.

- Shop regularly at the same stores. The proprietor or salespeople will get to know you, and you'll get preferential treatment.

- Patronize stores and catalogs from which you can order by telephone. Call stores at 10 A.M., before they get busy. Call catalogs during off-peak times, Wednesday at 9 P.M. instead of Monday morning, for example (better yet, send faxes).

- Be organized before the call:

    —Have pen and paper handy.

    —List any questions you have about the product.

    —If ordering from a catalog, flag pages and highlight or circle item numbers.

    —Have your credit card out.

    —Ask for the sales representative's name (often they tell you at the beginning of the call), and you'll get better service.

- Take advantage of pickup and delivery services. Even if there is a slight charge, the convenience is usually worth it.

- When shopping for major items such as furniture:

    —Plan on at least one shopping trip for research, another to buy.

    —Always carry a tape measure and paint chips or swatches.

    —Take along a camera to jog your memory and to compare items you're considering. Note size, dimensions, and material on the back of the picture and store in your Household Notebook.

- Is a contractor or decorator purchasing items for you? Keep a record on file of the name and address of the original supplier (of kitchen tile, living room drapery fabric, etc.), in case you need to replace anything.

- Shop sales to save money (50 percent and more) on holiday supplies, children's clothing, white sales, etc.

MONEY SAVER!

CLUTTER CONTROL

- If the clutter has finally gotten you down, start with a ten-minute room make-over:

  —Get a large basket and load up all items that don't belong.

  —Stack magazines.

  —Fluff pillows.

  —Vacuum if necessary.

- Or for a more thorough job:

  —Start by clearing the floor, one section at a time, working systematically.

  —Group like things together.

  —Save papers to sort later.

  —As you work, decide to save, donate, or toss, and put items in the appropriate piles. If the items are to be saved, put them away: videotapes in videotape drawer, books on bookshelf, games in closet.

- If you're reorganizing an entire room, you may not be able to finish in one session. Make certain that before you quit for the day one section of the room shows tremendous improvement. It will be your inspiration to continue the next day. And before you quit, clear the floor of the "reorganizing clutter" (piles to donate, garbage bag, etc.) so that you are leaving the area as neat as possible.

- To maintain a decluttered room:

  —Show family members the systems you've created. Teach them where to put things.

  —Heavily used rooms such as bedrooms and family rooms need to be picked up and organized daily. Try to spend at least 15 minutes per day tidying up. The more consistent you are, the less time you'll need to spend at the end of the week.

- A final "clutter" tip: Display items can become clutter. Like a museum, your home should have a "permanent" collection (things you adore), and a rotating "exhibit" of items you bring out for a while and then replace with something else.

  —Walk through your house at least once a year (January is a time), and take down novelty items: (a) you don't like any more; (b) that have lost their emotional significance; (c) you are temporarily tired of.

  —Rearrange the things you love and want to display. You'll enjoy the items in new locations because they'll no longer be part of the background you've grown accustomed to.

A HOME AWAY FROM HOME: the well-organized car

■ For most families today, cars have become extensions of our homes. Here's what you need for a well-organized car:

—Local maps

—Change for tolls and parking

—Spare sunglasses

—Folding umbrella

—Wastebasket

—Backseat car organizer for passenger paraphernalia

—Window scraper in winter; window cover in summer

—Window cleaner and paper towels

—Safety equipment (first-aid kit, white handkerchief for using as distress signal, flares, a tire jack, tools, and a blanket) should be stored in a canvas bag in the trunk.

■ Add to your supplies the new instant "inflate your tire" product sold in cans at car-supply stores. In an emergency it will get you a little farther on a low or flat tire.

■ Dog owners should keep a spare leash in the car.

■ In your Household Notebook note dates for tune-ups, oil changes, tire rotation, and put these dates on your calendar.

ABOUT THE AUTHORS

RONNI EISENBERG, author of *Organize Yourself!*, has given a multitude of workshops, lectures, and demonstrations across the country on how to get organized. She lives and works in Westport, Connecticut, with her husband and three children.

KATE KELLY, who co-authors Ronni's books, is a professional writer who owns and operates her own publishing business. She lives in Westchester County, New York, with her husband and three children.